LET GO AND GROW

Recovery for Adult Children
of Alcoholics

Robert J. Ackerman, Ph.D.
Indiana University of Pennsylvania

Health Communications, Inc.
Pompano Beach, Florida

Robert J. Ackerman, Ph.D.
Indiana University of Pennsylvania
Indiana, Pennsylvania

Library of Congress Cataloging-in-Publication Data

Ackerman, Robert J.
  Let go and grow.

  1. Adult children of alcoholics — United States
— Psychology. I. Title.
HV5132.A26 1987   362.2'92   87-21130
ISBN 0-932194-51-6

©1987   Robert J. Ackerman

ISBN 0-932194-51-6

Cover design by Reta Kaufman

Published by Health Communications, Inc.
        1721 Blount Road
        Pompano Beach, Florida 33069

Acknowledgments

I would like to thank the more than one thousand adults who participated in the study upon which much of this book is based. Your willingness to share yourself is greatly appreciated. A special thank you is due Joyce Tang for her assistance in processing questionnaires and to Georgia Springer for her administrative support. I am especially indebted to Judy Michaels, my research assistant on this project, and for her endless hours of support and hard work. Her contributions to this book are enormous.

To Oliver Ford, for editorial expertise and ideas I owe a special thank you. His support of my work and his encouragement are deeply appreciated. I wish to thank Charles Bertness and Mark Staszkiewicz, of the Instructional Research Program, of Indiana University of Pennsylvania for their research and computer expertise. Finally, I want to acknowledge the support of the Graduate School and the Faculty Research Associate Program of Indiana University of Pennsylvania without which this project would not have been possible.

Dedication
to
Kimberly,
Jason and Robert

Contents

Tables

---

* This table is reprinted by permission of Thomas Perrin from the pamphlet "I am an Adult Child of an Alcoholic", Thomas W. Perrin, Inc, 1983.

1

Survive Now, Heal Later

The majority of adult children of alcoholics whom I have met consider themselves to be survivors. They may not admit it openly, but perhaps secretly they are even proud of the fact that they are survivors. For example, without their levels of resilience where would they be now? If it were not for their ability to take control, accomplish tasks at an early age and only depend upon themselves, how could they have survived childhood?

For the now grown-up adult child of the alcoholic, however, survival is no longer the issue. The question is what kind of survivors are they today? For the adult child of the alcoholic, the specific question might be: are you a survivor who is able to achieve positive emotional intimacy? Or are you one who is resentful, angry or distrustful? Are you a survivor who abuses substances, or have you married someone who is addicted? Are you capable of being a healthy parent? Or are you a survivor who in spite of your negative childhood experiences, has been able to make the transition into a positive adulthood and become a healthy and fully functioning person?

Obviously, no one individual is just one of these types, but rather possesses a diversity of survival characteristics. Whatever combination you may possess, it is likely you survived under an unspoken motto of "survive now and heal later" while you were growing up. As an adult today, however, later is "now", and you are confronted with resolving many issues that may have been postponed. The resolution of these issues is a process which will require time, energy and understanding.

The Recovery Process

Recovery is a journey, not a destination. It is a process, not an accomplishment, a process that will require the adult child to learn to let go of the past and any negative influences, allowing oneself to grow. The best that some adult children will be able to achieve will be to let go of the past. They will achieve a position of emotional neutrality. Other adult children will be able to go beyond neutrality and grow, improve their lives and become the person they choose to be. A great part of recovery and letting go will be contingent on the adult child's ability to make peace in many areas of his or her life.

For example, some adult children will need to make peace with the past, with their parent or parents, with any siblings, with their spouses, with their own children and, most importantly, with themselves. It is difficult to make peace with others and achieve acceptance when one is still not at peace with oneself. Thus "inner" peace will become the key to achieving outer peace with those around you. Additionally, the achieving of inner peace does not depend on anyone else. Even if outer contentment is not achievable, the adult child still will have made a journey that has enabled him or her not only to achieve forgiveness and acceptance, but also to like himself or herself as he or she is.

How difficult the journey will be depends upon the impact of parental alcoholism and the ability of the adult child to achieve positive emotional intimacy in his or her life. This will require removing many known and unknown barriers. Thus the adult child may face the dilemma of wanting to grow, but not knowing how.

What then is the adult child to do who wants to overcome the negative effects of childhood, but who is still emotionally attached to the alcoholic family and thus, knowingly or unknowingly, is holding onto patterns of behaviors that inhibit growth? Additionally, what is the adult child to do when many of the people from the adult's childhood will not or cannot erase the issues and earlier behaviors? Many individuals who affect us negatively cannot or will not return to undo the damage. Therefore, the adult child is confronted with a choice of maintaining the "eternal yesterday" of their youth and allowing it to dominate their adult lives or choosing the positive option to *Let Go and Grow.*

If you are an adult child who has held on too long to the negative impacts and emotions experienced as a child, ask yourself what are you holding on to and why are you holding on? Are you waiting for someone else to come and take these things away? Are you fearful of what will happen if you let go? If you do absolutely nothing, you can be sure of one thing — that absolutely nothing will happen. If your life is to improve, *you* must lead the change, *you* must invest energy in yourself and *you* must find support to do this. You do not have to do this alone, however. There are more than 28 million adult children of alcoholics (ACoAs) in this country, so ACoAs do not need to be alone unless they choose to be. Nor can you avoid making a choice: either you do nothing or you *Let Go and Grow.*

Types of Recovery Journeys

Not all adult children, however, will take nor need to take the same journey of recovery from childhood experiences. Just as there are different types of adult survivors, there are also differences in recovery. Nor will all adult children all need to resolve the same issues. In recovery, there is "recovery lag". This means that not all parts of the individual will need the same depth of intervention and that not all parts of the adult child will recover at the same rate. Some issues will be easily worked through by affirmation and group support. Other issues will require longer periods of understanding and a more in-depth approach to resolution.

Additionally, I do not accept that all adult children of alcoholics are dominated by totally dysfunctional behaviors or feelings. How could people who were able to survive be totally dysfunctional? Certainly they must have had functional behaviors to survive. It is ironic that many adult children of alcoholics do not consider or appreciate their strengths that may have been learned in childhood, albeit negatively, as possible assets to assist their recovery in adulthood. Many survival skills do not need to be abandoned after the survival period is over.

(4) LET GO AND GROW

These very skills can become a repertoire of behaviors to help recover from the experience. There are many positive behaviors and emotions possessed by adult children of alcoholics. Assessing these will require insight and understanding, and more importantly, will require the understanding that not all adult children of alcoholics will possess the same positive and negative characteristics. Just as there are many differences among adults in general so are there differences in adult children of alcoholics.

For example, some adult children become alcoholics themselves but others do not. Some adult children marry spouses who eventually become alcoholics yet others do not. Some adult children become excellent parents and others have difficulty in child-rearing. Some adult children are able to achieve positive attitudes about their lives yet others cannot. Finally, some adult children possess the abilities to achieve positive emotional intimacy whereas others cannot. Although there may be many common patterns among adult children of alcoholics, each person is unique.

Personality Characteristics

What particular personality characteristics or behaviors do you possess? Answer the questions in Table 1.1 to assess some of your personality characteristics. It is obvious that not every adult child of an alcoholic will possess the same personality traits or to the same degree. Also many adults who are not adult children of alcoholics will identify with these same characteristics. What may be different between ACoAs and adults in general is the degree to which each possesses or does not possess any of these characteristics and the combination of them. The characteristics in 1.1 have been identified in clinical observations of adult children of alcoholics made by professionals. Even though these characteristics may be found both in adult children and adults in general, not only may the degree to which the characteristics found in each group differ, but also the motivation for the development of the behavior. That is, each group may appear to exhibit similar behaviors, but the reasons for learning the behavior and for maintaining the behavior may be very different for ACoAs than for other adults. For the child of an alcoholic, the behavior may have been learned as an adaptive response to a dysfunctional situation, whereas adults reared in a functional family may possess the same characteristics, but for different reasons and to lesser degrees.

Table 1.1*
Adult Personality Characteristics

(Indicate how often you engage in the following behaviors, using the scale to rate your responses)

5 = Always, 4 = Often, 3 = Sometimes, 2 = Seldom, 1 = Never

1. I guess at what is normal. _____
2. I have difficulty following projects through to completion. _____
3. I lie when it would be just as easy to tell the truth. _____
4. I judge myself without mercy. _____
5. I have difficulty having fun. _____
6. I take myself very seriously. _____
7. I have difficulty with intimate relationships. _____
8. I overreact to changes over which I have no control. _____
9. I feel different from other people. _____
10. I constantly seek approval and affirmation. _____
11. I am either super responsible or irresponsible. _____
12. I am extremely loyal even in the face of evidence that the loyalty is undeserved. _____
13. I look for immediate as opposed to deferred gratification. _____
14. I lock myself into a course of action without serious consideration to alternate choices or consequences. _____
15. I seek tension and crisis and then complain. _____
16. I avoid conflict or aggravate it but rarely deal with it. _____
17. I fear rejection and abandonment yet I reject others. _____
18. I fear failure but have difficulty handling success. _____
19. I fear criticism and judgment yet I criticize others. _____
20. I manage my time poorly and do not set my priorities in a way that works well for me. _____

(* Developed by R. Ackerman with J. Woititz, T. Perrin, 1985)

In the following section you can compare your answers to how adult children and adults in general responded to the questions in Table 1.1. These responses are based on information gathered from more than one thousand adults, with an equal distribution between adult children of alcoholics and adults in general. This data was gathered from a national study conducted by the author. The complete research and the methodological issues are addressed in Appendix A (Ackerman, 1986).

Key: ACoA = Adult Children of Alcoholics
ADULTS = Adults Who Did Not Have Alcoholic
Parent/s

Characteristic 1

I guess at what is normal.

Score: ACoA *3.13* ADULTS *2.51*

This characteristic is obviously more relevant for someone who has not been raised in a normal family situation. If you come from a normal family, there is no need to guess at what is normal because you have lived it. Many children of alcoholics do not want others to know that their house is different and, therefore, they have a motivation or an emotional reason for wanting to convince others that they are the same as everyone else. Since the child of the alcoholic often lacks exposure to any modeling of normal behavior, he or she must guess at what is normal. For ACoAs, this guessing at what is normal may have started in their family of origin, but often has been carried over into other periods of their lives so they continue to guess about how to be "normal" spouses, friends, parents or people.

Characteristic 2

I have difficulty following projects through to completion.

Score: ACoA *2.77* ADULTS *2.42*

Most of these characteristics for adult children have their origins in childhood and are carried over into adulthood. This characteristic is a good example of such a carry-over. The accomplishments and presence in the home of many children of alcoholics is often secondary to the alcoholism and the negative spouse relationship. Therefore, many adult children can remember very little attention being paid to their accomplishments, so their motivation for completion declined with the lack of parental response. Other adult children, however, may remember that it was difficult to complete tasks because of the constant interruptions or family disruptions which impeded completion of tasks. Still other adult children may not identify with this characteristic at all since it was through the completion of tasks that they received recognition. What may have hampered these adult children was that it took increasingly elaborate tasks to attract attention, and thus completion became more difficult as the difficulty of the task increased.

Characteristic 3

I lie when it would be just as easy to tell the truth.

Score: ACoA 2.21 ADULTS 1.81

Many of these characteristics are related to each other. This characteristic could be related to number one in that not only might you guess at what is normal, but also you would like others to think that you are. Therefore you might lie not only to convince them, but also to protect yourself from exposure. After a while, the lying becomes a part of your manner of communicating with others. Additionally, you may not even perceive the lying as negative because it is a defense mechanism for protection. The adult child may draw a distinct perception between lying that is negative as opposed to lying that "really" isn't lying but only self-protection. Yet another way of perceiving this behavior is a continuation of the pattern your parents set when they told you one thing and did another. One of the most common traits in alcoholic families is mixed messages of communication. The parents live one way and instruct the children not to tell anyone or ask the child to deny to outsiders whatever he or she sees. Perhaps for some adult children the most enduring lie originated when everyone in the family denied that anything was wrong, yet no one felt right.

Characteristic 4

I judge myself without mercy.

Score: ACoA   3.50   *ADULTS*   2.90

Many adult children perceive that perfection is the only acceptable standard of performance and evaluation. Although there are many adults without alcoholic parents who are perfectionists, adult children may possess different motivations for self-perfection. This may stem from a feeling that it is imperative to please everyone in order to keep peace in the house. Since this can never be achieved on more than a very short-term basis, the child becomes increasingly critical of himself or herself for not being able to be successful. These unrealistic standards of performance and evaluation are carried over by many adult children. Some evaluate all of their behavior against a standard of 101%. That is, for anything to be even acceptable, let alone outstanding or great, it must be 100% perfect; being short by even 1% makes it all wrong. Curiously, others' imperfections may not bother adult children at all, despite the unrealistic standards they set for themselves. They often will set lower standards of acceptable perfomances in others, yet judge themselves without mercy. Thus many adult children preserve a double standard of performance evaluation, unconsciously maintaining the same patterns of double or mixed messages which they "survived" as children. This only adds to problems of isolation and unnecessary feelings of inadequacy for adult children who consistently expect more from themselves than they do from others. Are adult children with this characteristic saying that they can help others achieve others' needs, but because of their impossibly high standards, others cannot help them achieve? Perhaps they thus survive the fear of failing as measured by standards for which they have no norms and which they have never understood.

Characteristic 5

I have difficulty having fun.

Score: ACoA   3.10   *ADULTS*   2.42

The motivation for this characteristic for adult children may have many origins and may affect only some adult children.

One of the things missing in the lives of many children of alcoholics is family fun. Much energy is expended in surviving, so there is none left for enjoyment. It may be difficult to let yourself go when you feel a strong need to be in control of your emotions. For others, having fun is difficult to learn while growing up in very seriously negative situations.

Having fun requires relaxing one's defenses and being vulnerable, something many adult children find difficult; perhaps because their continued survival has required and conditioned them to continual vigilance. Many adult children have developed extraordinary senses of humor, but have difficulty relaxing and having fun. Often their humor is extremely sarcastic or self-directed. Many famous comedians and comediennes in our society come from very dysfunctional family backgrounds. They possess the ability to make others laugh, but may not be able to experience fun or happiness themselves.

Another reason for this characteristic may simply be that many adult children can remember not having time for fun while growing up, and, therefore, find it difficult today to develop or value this behavior.

I once observed a three-year-old child ask her grandmother to play a game on the living-room floor. The grandmother, who was the spouse of an alcoholic, replied to the child and to others in the room that "Grandmother doesn't play". Although this was not said to hurt the child, play may not have been possible for the grandmother. Play requires being receptive to unstructured experience and vulnerable to the unexpected. A lifetime as the spouse of an alcoholic, doubtless, had conditioned her to avoid situations she could not control. She had been rendered incapable of learning how to play, even with her own granddaughter. What she did not realize was that the child could have taught her how to play and that not only was it all right to have fun, but also that it was normal.

Characteristic 6

I take myself very seriously.

Score: ACoA   3.80   ADULTS   3.40

It is difficult to determine if taking yourself very seriously is more an adult characteristic in general or if, for children of alcoholics, it is a by-product from dysfunctional family relationships. This characteristic and the difficulty in having fun are probably related to each other. Therefore, many of the factors related to the difficulty of having fun are applicable to adult children who take themselves too seriously. Perhaps the motivation for this characteristic for the adult child is a carry-over from circumstances in childhood, which required the child to consistently act older than his or her age, and to engage in behaviors that were extremely mature. This pattern of adaptation may have demanded that the child abandon childhood behaviors too early and assume adult "serious" responsiblities too soon. Many adults raised in dysfunctional families express that one of their common feelings is that they "missed childhood". The adult child may have learned at a very early age the seriousness of alcoholism, parental discord and related issues in a dysfunctional family, issues which in turn led to the development of a very serious attitude not only about himself/herself, but about living in general.

Characteristic 7

I have difficulty with intimate relationships.

Score: ACoA   3.46   ADULTS   2.74

Of all the characteristics that one may develop from living in an alcoholic family, this characteristic has the greatest impact. Although adults in general will admit to having problems with intimate relationships, some adult children suffer from extreme difficulty in achieving positive emotional relationships in their lives. This may be particularly true for the adult child who was exposed not only to parental alcoholism, but also to high degrees of marital conflict among the parents. Research has indicated that children of alcoholics are far more upset by the negative relationships between their parents than they are by the drinking of the alcoholic (Cork, 1969).

It is difficult to learn how to achieve successful intimate relationships when you have been raised around negative ones. The adult child may not have been exposed to healthy adult relationships which could serve as models for future adult relationships.   Additionally, possessing many of the characteristics on this list to an extreme degree may contribute to problems in achieving intimacy. It not only would be difficult to be a fully functioning and healthy individual if you possessed most of these characteristics, it would also impede your ability to contribute and receive in a healthy relationship with another. What further complicates the intimacy problem for many adult children is that having positive intimate relationships is exactly what they are looking for and is exactly what they have always perceived that they would do when they developed their own adult relationships and families. But often they find that they may not possess the abilities to achieve the very intimacy for which they are looking.

Characteristic 8

I overreact to changes over which I have no control.

Score: ACoA   3.31   *ADULTS*   2.79

The motivation for this behavior for adult children does not pertain to overreaction as much as it relates to the need to maintain control over situations. In order to reduce family chaos and survive their family situation, adult children may have adapted by taking charge whenever possible. Many people are able to handle confusion and disorderly situations better if they can control the situation, thereby reducing their anxiety over the uncertainty they feel. Exposure to situations over which you have no control, however, may be even more stressful for adults who have learned to survive stress by seizing control. It may not be the changes which are causing stress for these adults, but their feelings that they have no control over the changes.

Characteristic 9

I feel different from other people.

Score: ACoA   3.21   *ADULTS*   2.75

A sense of personal uniqueness is not unusual for adults. After all, most of us feel that if everyone else was like us, the world would be fine. The motivation for adult children with this characteristic is obvious. That is, they were not raised like everyone else. Even in young children, the feeling of being different in the alcoholic home becomes apparent. As a matter of fact, it may be that the children of the alcoholic perceive that their homes are different long before they realize what is causing the difference.

For example, the young child may perceive that her house is different from those of her friends, but is too young to understand the dynamics of alcoholism. In time she may realize that the difference in her home makes negative differences in her life. Eventually she will discover what is causing the difference. The adult child may suffer from a feeling of estrangement from others even in normal situations and not understand the motivations for the feeling. This emotional isolation may contribute to his/her awareness of being less in control and thus increase the probability of feeling different.

Characteristic 10

I constantly seek approval and affirmation.

Score: ACoA   3.44   ADULTS   2.99

Not all adult children will identify with this behavior. This behavior is concerned not with recognition or approval of a task or one's performance, but is concerned with self-esteem and the validating of personal worth of the adult child. Some adult children became extremely competent at many tasks early in life. These accomplishments brought recognition, but more important it brought approval of what the children were doing and enabled them to control certain aspects of their lives. It was not the accomplishment that was important for the child, it was the approval, and usually this approval had to come from who was important to the child. What this approval indicated for many children of alcoholics was that they had a sense of worth which was related to accomplishments. This sense of worth provided a validation not only of the accomplishment, but of personal worth. Thus many adult children may have developed into "accomplishment or success junkies". Only through their successes were they able to have their worth as a person validated, and unfortunately this validation had to come from external sources rather than from the adult child.

The problem for many adult children who have this characteristic is summed up in the question, "If I am what I do, then who am I if I am not doing something?" They measure their personal worth by way of external approval for accomplishments, and they use indirect validation of these accomplishments as internal affirmation of their self-esteem. The adult child with this behavior either continues to seek accomplishment after accomplishment in order to maintain adequate self-esteem or must learn to provide affirmation of self-worth by other means. This obviously is the old saying of finding your self-concept not in what you do, but in who you are. This is difficult for people who are not at peace with themselves internally, thus for them external validation becomes a convenient alternative.

Characteristic 11

I am either super responsible or irresponsible.

Score: ACoA   *3.41*   *ADULTS*   *2.68*

For adult children this characteristic is an all or nothing behavior. Whether or not an adult child identifies with this behavior may depend upon how they adjusted to parental alcoholism, whether by becoming exceptionally competent individuals or by manifesting behaviors which led to irresponsibility and acting-out behaviors which became problematic. Additionally this behavior may be reflective of the alcoholic behavior with which the adult child grew up.

For example, many alcoholic parents perform their parenting duties from either of two extremes — treating people one way when they were sober and differently when drinking. This Jekyll-and-Hyde personality pattern is familiar to many adult children. When drinking the alcoholic would demonstrate irresponsible behavior to the child, and when sober would try to do all of the positive parenting at one time. On some occasions the adult child would be ignored or chastised, and then at other times be "overly" parented and loved.

Characteristic 12

I am extremely loyal even in the face of evidence that the loyalty is undeserved.

Score: ACoA   *3.32*   *ADULTS*   *3.04*

Is any relationship better than no relationship? Children of alcoholics, like other children in dysfunctional homes, may be faced with physical or emotional abandonment. Adult children may remember thinking about what would happen to them if something happened to the alcoholic or if the parental fighting led to a breakup of their parents. The motivation for extreme loyalty may come from several sources. It is one thing for you to say that the person with whom you live is causing problems; it is another thing for someone else to say so. Part of the reason for denial of alcoholism in families may be a sense of loyalty not to disclose "family business". Thus family members become enmeshed in many loyalty patterns that are negative before considering any negative implications from their undeserved loyalty.

Also the adult child of one alcoholic parent may have witnessed extreme loyalty by the non-alcoholic parent to his or her spouse, even when the non-alcoholic spouse was being treated unfairly. In cases of spouse abuse there often remains a sense of loyalty to the abuser, even though it obviously is undeserved. What causes this loyalty in dysfunctional families is not clear, but many adult children may develop a loyalty pattern that will remain strong even in dysfunctional relation-ships and thus will keep them in the relationship. Where loyalty is undeserved, the victims may deny that someone they are involved with would hurt them or they may deny the extent of the injury. Thus statements such as "he or she really is a good person, you just don't understand them" or "you don't know them the way I do" become common. Another motivation for undeserved loyalty may come from a low self-esteem. The loyal person feels that he or she does not deserve better or allows him/herself to be manipulated into being loyal.

Sharon Wegscheider-Cruse points out that to survive nonsense requires manipulation (Wegscheider-Cruse, 1978). In the alcoholic family manipulation is going on at two levels. First, the alcoholic will manipulate family members in order to continue with the alcoholic behavior. This may take the form of denial, cover-up, alibis, or verbal manipulation. Second, non-alcoholic family members will begin to manipu-late themselves to avoid "rocking the boat". They may suppress or subordinate normal family behaviors, individual requests, arguments or their own well-being in order to keep the peace. This is a form of loyalty with which the adult child may have lived without realizing that he or she was manipu-lated into undeserved loyalty.

Characteristic 13

I look for immediate as opposed to deferred gratification.

Score: ACoA   3.08   *ADULTS*   2.68

Some adult children will identify with this behavior more
than others. For adult children who were reared in a home of
severe inconsistency, immediacy and seizing the opportunity
for gratification may have been more of the norm in their
childhood. Not knowing how long something will last or if it
will come again may have increased their taking advantage of
it immediately. Adult children reared in a more consistent
manner may have had the opportunity to plan ahead more or
had the comfort of knowing that they could defer gratification. Since most alcoholic families are dominated by high
degrees of inconsistency, it would be expected that more adult
children would identify with immediate rather than deferred
gratification. For some this is true.

Other adult children, however, developed a pattern while
children of alcoholics consistently put themselves second,
thinking or consoling themselves with the thought that their
time would come later. This may be the motivation for many
adult children being more willing to help others than to help
themselves. Responses to this aspect of their lives as children
of alcoholics is a good example of how adult children do not
identify with or react to the same degree or even in the same
manner to the same experience as children.

Characteristic 14

*I lock myself into a course of action without serious considera-
tion of alternate choices or consequences.*

Score: ACoA   2.74   *ADULTS*   2.30

Is it possible that this characteristic helps to explain why so
many adult children find themselves in problem marriages?
This behavior is similar to the one where when many people
are faced with a crisis, they will choose the first solution that
appears viable as opposed to the best solution. Expediency
may take precedence over optimal choices. The motivation
for this may stem from the fact that many choices in the
alcoholic family are made solely to reduce the impact of

alcoholism, rather than to achieve what is best for the family members. Additionally, if this characteristic is related to immediate gratification of needs, then deliberation over choices is not likely. On the other hand, individuals who are used to putting themselves second may not seek the best choices but will settle for less or for whatever will work. Another motivation for this behavior could be found in communication styles. Often finding the best choice is facilitated by discussion with others. However, in families with poor communication patterns, decisions may be made in isolation with little sharing of information or opinions.

Characteristic 15

I seek tension and crisis and then complain.

Score: ACoA   2.54   *ADULTS*   2.10

How well can you handle it when things are quiet or normal? Are you waiting for the roof to cave in? Which do you handle better, success or crisis? When do you feel more alive, during normal periods or during a crisis? Are you an "excitement junkie"? Some adult children have become so used to living in crisis situations that crisis living almost becomes normal and normal living becomes difficult. The very absence of a crisis creates anxiety or tension. Some adult children feel that when things are fine, it is only a period between crises. Others may believe they felt most needed during stressful times.

Complaining about the situation may not be an act of discomfort with the situation. It may actually be a method of bringing attention to one's self about being in a crisis again and receiving recognition from others regarding how well you handle several things at one time. It is questionable, however, if adult children actually seek crisis or if much of their behavior merely puts them at a high risk for getting involved in a crisis situation. You may ask yourself "why is it always me?" when you should be asking "what is it about me that gets me into these situations?" Existing in tension and in crisis situations therefore may not be by choice, but rather by faulty design.

Characteristic 16

I avoid conflict or aggravate it, but rarely deal with it.

Score: ACoA   2.81   ADULTS   2.42

By now you may have noticed that many of these characteristics represent two extreme behaviors, thus representing
another form of "either/or" behavior for adult children. Some
adult children will be extremely fearful of any kind of conflict
and in fact will not only avoid, but will also spend much of
their energy in placating or mediating conflicts between
others. Helping others deal with their conflict may appear
generous of you initially, but is it another way for you to keep
from dealing with your own conflicts? "I'll help you and you
and you, but I won't let any of you help me" could become a
common statement. The adult child may have learned to fear
all conflicts between people and may have developed the idea
that positive relationships should be free of conflict. Therefore
a good relationship is equated with being conflict-free and a
problematic relationship, with open conflict. This becomes a
very unrealistic perception of healthy relationships, which is
only found in the movies, not in our lives. It recalls Eric Segal's
famous line from *Love Story* that "love means never having to
say you're sorry" (Segal, 1977). I would prefer to be in a
relationship with someone who has the ability and the
empathy to apologize in the face of conflict rather than avoid
it.

The opposite side of this behavior is found in individuals
who aggravate conflict. Anger and resentment are often two
feelings disproportionately found in adult children of
alcoholics. The sources of the anger may differ but the
outcome may lead to aggravating conflict with others and
particularly with those who are not the source of the original
conflict. You may grow up with an alcoholic parent and
become resentful and angry, yet direct your feelings towards
others and not towards the source of the anger. Anger towards
others is not dealing with the source of the feeling, and,
therefore, resolving the conflict is not only avoided but
postponed.

Some adult children may have consistently internalized the
chaos in their family and then later externalized it through
inappropriate behavior. This external behavior often contributed to conflict with others, but never allowed for the

discovery or alleviation of the original conflict. Adult children with this pattern may be easily recognized by others because they are like being around a human time-bomb just about to go off.

Characteristic 17

I fear rejection and abandonment, yet I reject others.

Score: ACoA   3.00   *ADULTS*   2.36

This behavior is typical of wanting to be needed and loved, but not being able to need and love others. Some adult children may find themselves not able to handle rejection and feel a tremendous sense of abandonment when it occurs. At the same time they are not able to get close to others if they are consistently rejecting others. This rejection may be for a variety of reasons, ranging from low self-esteem to the fear of being hurt. Others may feel a great need to be accepted because they have always felt different and they want to be normal. It is ironic, however, that they may reject the normal people around them because these people are different and "would not understand them".

Some adult children may be extremely fearful of abandonment because this is one of the greatest childhood fears of children. Since many behaviors of adult children are carried over from childhood, the fear of abandonment may be even more powerful for children raised in homes that were highly dysfunctional, with this fear being raised more often than in normal families.

Characteristic 18

I fear failure, but have difficulty handling success.

Score: ACoA   3.37   *ADULTS*   2.77

Have you ever succeeded, not because of your desire for success, but because of your fear of failure? This characteristic is associated with two issues: fear of failure and handling of success. Many adult children are extremely successful professionals, but are constantly afraid of failure and therefore push themselves excessively in order to avoid failing. It is this avoidance that indirectly produces the success.

In other words they may be doing all of the right things, but for the wrong reasons. It appears to others that they are highly successful, but their self-esteem may be more related to failure avoidance than success acceptance. Ironically, many adult children are told how competent they are by others, but maintain a low self-concept of themselves.

Other adult children may have difficulty handling success. They work towards accomplishing their goals or towards having healthy relationships and at the same time expect the world to cave in around them if they are successful. For example, the adult child in quest of a truly healthy and meaningful relationship finds one, and then what happens? Does he or she enjoy the relationship and feel that he or she deserves to be in a healthy relationship, or does he or she begin to sabotage the success and begin to prepare for failure, thus creating a self-fulfilling prophecy that "even if I find a good relationship, it won't last".

Handling success may be analogous to handling a compliment. When someone tells you that you look nice, do you say "thank you" or do you push the compliment aside with "oh, this old thing" or "I bought this on sale" or "it was a gift"? Handling true success requires being able to balance the acceptance of failure and success in the same person. Additionally, the motivations for success should not be dependent upon avoiding failure. Both success and failure are normal. If you fear failure, it is possible that you also fear success.

Characteristic 19

I fear criticism and judgment, yet I criticize others.

Score: ACoA   3.14   ADULTS   2.67

Adult children who have low self-concepts may identify with this characteristic the most. If your self-concept is fragile or low, it does not take much criticism or negative judgment to destroy it. Therefore, any criticism or judgment is to be avoided. This is especially true if you take the criticism personally. That is, although it may be your works or actions that are criticized, you interpret it as a criticism of the kind of person that you are. Additionally, if you possess many of the other characteristics of perfectionism — over-seriousness, extreme self-criticism, approval-seeking and loyalty — you may be extremely sensitive, not only to outside criticism, but also to internalizing it to be a reflection on yourself.

Criticizing others may have many motivations. These may range from needing to find fault with others to justify your own faults, to being envious of others who seem to have it all together. It is less painful for you to see these people if you can find an error in their "perfect life".

Additionally, criticizing others may be motivated by being reared in a situation where the negative was always pointed out. Therefore, rather than seeing the positive aspects of any situation, the adult child with this motivation will concentrate on the potential weaknesses. This pattern of criticism may have been learned from always expecting the worst. In order to prepare for these expectations, one learned to identify them in most situations. These identifying statements could be voiced as criticism, but for the adult child they may be the constant frame of reference from which the ACoA normally views behaviors and situations. Thus criticism of others may not be so much of a direct criticism of another, as it may be an indirect way for the adult child to prepare himself or herself for potential problems and to fulfill his or her own low expectations.

Characteristic 20

I manage my time poorly and do not set priorities in a way that works well for me.

Score: ACoA   2.83   ADULTS   2.58

Why do adult children demonstrate this characteristic? Some of the motivation may be better understood by considering how they establish priorities. It is possible that putting others' needs first continually will interrupt their own priorities, but more importantly this characteristic may develop from the inability of some adult children to say "no" to others. Their reasons for doing this may come from not being able to express their own needs, putting their own needs second or feeling that if they tell others "no" they would be rejected. However, not being able to tell others "no" means

Table 1.2

Comparison of Adult Personality Characteristics Between Adult Children of Alcoholic and Non-Alcoholic Parents

Score
5 = Always, 4 = Often, 3 = Sometimes, 2 = Seldom, 1 = Never

	ACoA	ADULTS
1. I guess at what is normal.	3.13	2.51
2. I have difficulty following projects through to completion.	2.77	2.42
3. I lie when it would be just as easy to tell the truth.	2.21	1.81
4. I judge myself without mercy.	3.50	2.90
5. I have difficulty having fun.	3.10	2.42
6. I take myself very seriously.	3.80	3.40
7. I have difficulty with intimate relationships.	3.46	2.74
8. I overreact to changes over which I have no control.	3.31	2.79
9. I feel different from other people.	3.21	2.75
10. I constantly seek approval and affirmation.	3.44	2.99
11. I am either super responsible or irresponsible.	3.41	2.68
12. I am extremely loyal even in the face of evidence that the loyalty is undeserved.	3.32	3.04
13. I look for immediate as opposed to deferred gratification.	3.08	2.68
14. I lock myself into a course of action without serious consideration to alternate choices or consequences.	2.74	2.30
15. I seek tension and crisis and then complain.	2.54	2.10
16. I avoid conflict or aggravate it but rarely deal with it.	2.81	2.42
17. I fear rejection and abandonment yet I reject others.	3.00	2.36
18. I fear failure but have difficulty handling success.	3.37	2.77
19. I fear criticism and judgment yet I criticize others.	3.14	2.67
20. I manage my time poorly and do not set my priorities in a way that works well for me.	2.83	2.58
TOTAL	62.17	52.33

that they are saying "yes" to others' demands on their time and emotions. This may occur at the expense of their own priorities.

Have you ever felt that you are constantly doing everything for everyone else and nothing for yourself? Do you put yourself in situations by not being able to say no because you feel guilty if you do? If so, then you are having your time managed by others' demands, rather than meeting your own needs, and perhaps you are beginning to resent the fact that you never have time for yourself. Obviously, helping others is a positive characteristic, but if carried to extremes, the others are helping themselves to you. The adult child in this situation must be able to establish and maintain a balanced set of priorities. This will require learning to say no when appropriate and learning to feel comfortable in saying no. It will also require developing a healthy sense of being able to meet one's own needs and then setting priorities and managing the areas in one's life appropriately.

In Table 1.2 the degree to which each characteristic is found in adult children of alcoholics is compared to adults who did not have an alcoholic parent (Table 1.2). One of the most notable differences is that on each characteristic adult children scored higher, although the range of differences between each score varied.

The differences on each item occurred in ranges and demonstrated that all adults share some of these characteristics to one degree or another. It is exactly the differences in degrees of each of these personality characteristics that separate adult children from adults in general. In her book *Adult Children of Alcoholics* Janet Woititz points out that adult children of alcoholics differ from other adults by the degree of personality characteristics rather than possessing different ones (Woititz, 1983). Not only does the degree of the characteristic differ, but also the characteristics adult children and adults, in general, possess the most may differ. For example, the five characteristics that adult children indicated that they possessed the most were:

1. I take myself very seriously
2. I judge myself without mercy
3. I have difficulty with intimate relationships
4. I constantly seek approval and affirmation
5. I am either super responsible or irresponsible

For other adults the characteristics identified with the most were:

1. I take myself very seriously
2. I am extremely loyal even in the face of evidence that the loyalty is undeserved
3. I constantly seek approval and affirmation
4. I judge myself without mercy
5. I overreact to changes over which I have no control

It is obvious that both adult children and other adults share some of the same characteristics above. Additionally, there are some differences which stand out more between these two groups. For example, the five characteristics that had the greatest range of differences (thus, those that adult children were far more concerned with than other adults) were:

1. I am either super responsible or irresponsible
2. I have difficulty with intimate relationships
3. I have difficulty having fun
4. I fear rejection and abandonment, yet I reject others
5. I guess at what is normal

Do these sound familiar to you? In many groups of adult children of alcoholics, the themes of intimacy, inability to have fun and taking yourself too seriously, fear of rejection, accepting too much responsibility and guessing at what is normal dominate the feelings of many of the participants. However, not all characteristics of adult children are attributable to being children of alcoholics. Some of these characteristics obviously are part of being an adult, but the adult child may possess them to a greater degree. On the other hand, not all behaviors in adult children can be directly associated with exposure to active alcoholism.

Alcoholizing Personality Characteristics

How can you know which personality traits you possess are attributable to being the child of an alcoholic? Are all your traits due to exposure to active alcoholism? It is possible that only some of your personality was influenced by being raised in an alcoholic family. It is obvious that for adult children of alcoholics their personalities are combinations of all of the above factors. In many alcoholic families, however, there is a tendency to blame all behaviors, in particular the negative ones, on alcoholism. Alcoholism in a parent or parents cannot account for all of the personality characteristics in children of alcoholics.

In most alcoholic families the longer the drinking continues, the higher the probability that more problems are blamed on the drinking. In one way or another everything gets related to alcoholism, including the personality development of the children and particularly if family members become over-whelmed with an "alcoholized" identity. It is very important for the adult child to be able to distinguish between personality characteristics that were strongly influenced by having had an alcoholic parent and those characteristics that the adult child developed unrelated from this influence.

Additionally for the adult child in recovery, it is important not to confuse normal developmental problems of adulthood with being an adult child. Remember that all adults have problems or concerns with relationships, intimacy, parenting, self-esteem, et cetera, and what may distinguish the adult child from other adults is only the degree to which one has these characteristics.

Finally, not all adult problems or feelings are caused by the same source. Feelings of inadequacy or low self-esteem may have been caused by a variety of conditions. Likewise, being exceptionally competent and successful can be caused both by positive and negative emotional motivations. Bruce D. Baldwin attributes success to many different motivations (Baldwin, 1985).

To assess some of your own characteristics, answer the questions in the quiz in Table 1.3.

If you said "yes" to several of the questions in Table 1.3 you may have what Baldwin describes as the "driven personality". Many adult children of alcoholics may identify with some of the driven personality characteristics. However, these characteristics, unlike the ones in Table 1.2, are not derived from exposure to an alcoholic parent. Baldwin thinks that typically they are developed in childhood from four patterns that he labels as overdrive patterns. These patterns are:
  1. Exclusive reinforcement for achievement
  2. The push for perfection
  3. Compensation for adolescent social insecurity
  4. Fear of childhood poverty and deprivation

Table 1.3

Personality Test

	YES	NO	
1.	_____	_____	You are fiercely independent and resist needing others emotionally or for other kinds of help.
2.	_____	_____	Whenever you get a bit of free time, you fill it up with work instead of using it to relax and enjoy yourself.
3.	_____	_____	You have very high standards for your work, and you arbitrarily impose those same standards on others, even when it is not necessary.
4.	_____	_____	You are always in a hurry and consequently very impatient with others because you have so many things to get done — now!
5.	_____	_____	You have a bad habit of putting off good times, relaxation and taking care of yourself until "later".
6.	_____	_____	You compete constantly, and your competiveness has a vicious streak that is very apparent to others.
7.	_____	_____	No matter what you are doing, you always have to have a "product" to show that justifies the time spent.
8.	_____	_____	When someone needs you emotionally, it is difficult for you to be empathetic because you want to solve the problems for him or her instead.
9.	_____	_____	You do not handle failure well, and such experiences, no matter how trivial, have a disproportionate impact on your self-esteem.
10.	_____	_____	You gravitate toward others who are workaholics like you, and then you compete with them even when at leisure.
11.	_____	_____	You need to be always in control of people or situations, and when your control is threatened, you become angry and defensive.
12.	_____	_____	You constantly overextend yourself emotionally, physically and financially because of your "bigger is always better" philosophy.

Thus it appears that many adults possessing these characteristics are extremely successful. However, they may in fact be doing all of the right things but for the wrong reasons. Again it is the emotional motivation for the behaviors that are critical. This is especially true for the adult child who feels empty, troubled or incapable of success in relationships. It is obvious from Table 1.3 that adult children of alcoholics are not the only adults who are concerned about resolving personal problems and leading fulfilling lives. What separates the adult child from other adults are the motivations for his or her behaviors, even though on the surface the behaviors may appear to be the same as other adults, and particularly other adults who were raised in dysfunctional families.

In fact one of the factors that may be giving such support to the adult children of alcoholics' movement is that many adults who were not raised in alcoholic families but were raised in other types of dysfunctional families are identifying with adult children of alcoholic issues. This identification should tell us at least two things. One, not all problems faced by adult children of alcoholics are unique only to those raised with alcoholic parents, and second, not all problems for children of alcoholics are produced exclusively from exposure to parental alcoholism.

Adult children of alcoholics are children who were raised in dysfunctional families. They share one common variable of having at least one alcoholic parent, but their diversity of personalities and their diversity of issues must be appreciated. Additionally, the adult child must realize that he or she will have many characteristics that may be similar to other adult children of alcoholics, but he or she may also share characteristics with others from different types of dysfunctional families.

Finally, not all problems for adult children in recovery are related to alcohol. The adult in recovery will need to assess which problems have their emotional origins in exposure to parental alcoholism, which problems are associated with being an adult and which problems are a combination of both. Although the adult children may make similar journeys along the road to recovery, each must be free to understand that not all will need to take the same paths, that some paths will not take as long as others and that some paths will be emotionally easier than others.

2

Why Adult Children Are Not All The Same°

Although adult children of alcoholics may share many similar experiences from having grown up in an alcoholic family, they are not all affected in the same way. One adult child may be devastated by the parental alcoholism, another becomes withdrawn and isolated and another survives well and emerges with fewer problems. Sometimes only one of the children in a family will accept or acknowledge the alcoholism, while others continue to deny not only the alcoholism but also that they were at all affected.

It is perhaps ironic that I have met so many adult children of alcoholics whose brothers and sisters are not adult children of alcoholics! To understand these differences one needs to consider the intervening variables in their experiences as the child of an alcoholic. These may include the degree of alcoholism experienced, the type and kind of alcoholic in the

°This chapter is based on the book Same House, Different Homes by Robert J. Ackerman. Health Communications, 1987.

family, the child's perception of the experience, the child's resiliency to stress, the gender of the alcoholic and the child, the age at which the adult child was exposed to alcoholism, any positive offsetting factors while growing up and any cultural considerations and implications. The different effects of these variables are not limited to childhood, but will manifest themselves in a variety of ways in the adult later. Obviously, many of the concerns and behaviors of adult children today were caused by their experiences in childhood. Therefore, the following variables are discussed not only as they may have affected you while you were growing up, but also as they may be affecting you today.

1. Degree of Alcoholism

Consideration of the degree of alcoholism found in the alcoholic assesses how significantly the alcoholism affected the ability of the parent while the adult child was growing up. For the child of the alcoholic, as for all children in general, the effectiveness of their parents as parents will be the factor in their relationship that will affect the child most. Although a parent may be alcoholic, he or she is first and foremost a parent to the child. How the alcoholic adult fulfills the parental role affects children more than the drinking. After all, if the drinking were not leading to dysfunctional behaviors, no one would be upset with the drinking. It is the inability of the alcoholic parent to fulfill his or her various parental roles successfully that become detrimental to those children around the alcoholic.

All adults occupy several roles simultaneously, but some of these roles are more critical than others. Most adults identify with a particular role that they fulfill more than others. This can be called the "master status" role. Additionally, others see the adult from the particular role which is most important to the observer. For children the adult caretaker in their lives occupies the master status role of parent.

If the adult next door is an alcoholic, it is very different from your own parent being alcoholic, because the adult next door does not occupy the same master status for you. Thus, for the child growing up, the question is how does this alcoholism affect the quality of child care?

For example, many alcoholics may be able to function outside of their family and maintain friends, jobs, et cetera, but not be able to function appropriately as a parent. In fact, it would not be uncommon for some adult children to remember and resent that the alcoholic parent was nice to everyone but his or her own family. Other adult children may feel that the parent tried to parent effectively, but was not able to meet the emotional needs of the children. The role impairment due to alcoholism that is most significant for children of alcoholics obviously is the impairment of the role of the alcoholic as parent.

2. The Type Or Kind of Alcoholic

Not all alcoholic parents act the same, nor fulfill their parental roles the same. To assess the different impacts on adult children, one should examine the different behavioral and parenting styles of the alcoholic parents. The expression, *type of alcoholic* refers to the personality type, whereas *kind of alcoholic* refers to the kinds of behaviors that the alcoholic parent engaged in, particularly when he or she was drinking.

Although one could argue that personality and behavior are the same, for the sake of argument let's look at them separately. Young children seem to be able to do this. The child may say, "I can't stand it when my mother is drinking" or "I hate it when my dad is drunk," but that does not mean that the child can't stand mother or hates dad. The child is able to separate the person from the behavior.

In many alcoholic families family members distinguish between alcohol behavior and sober behavior by such statements as "he (or she) are the greatest person when he (or she) is sober, but watch out for him (her) when he (she) is drinking". It is as if they understand that under the influence of alcohol, the parent undergoes a personality change. These changes may have increased the problems in childhood for adult children because of the amount and variety of role inconsistency in the alcoholic parent to whom they were exposed.

In Table 2.1 the different types of behavior in the alcoholic parent are identified, along with the prevalence of each noted by adult children of alcoholics. This table not only illustrates the differences in behaviors found among alcoholics when drinking, but also that the adult children identified even more than one behavior occurring in the same alcoholic. These different behaviors within the same individual further confuse the role inconsistency already being experienced in the family.

Table 2.1

**Alcoholic's Behavior When Drinking as Identified by
Adult Children of Alcoholics**

Type of Behavior*	Identified in Alcoholic Parent (Percentage of Yes Responses)
Verbally Belligerent	49.0%
Offensive	41.5
Passive	31.0
Carefree	13.5
Other	14.3

More than one behavior could be identified

As indicated in the above table, verbal belligerence was the most common form of behavior identified by adult children in their alcoholic parents. This behavior was followed by offensive behavior which could have ranged from embarrassment to abuse. The next most commonly identified behavior was passivity in the alcoholic, followed by being carefree and other forms of behavior. It is obvious that not only does alcoholism profoundly affect the adult child, but also the forms of behaviors associated with the alcoholic in and of themselves may be extremely difficult behaviors to tolerate. Thus the adult child may have learned to adapt to alcoholism and to highly undesirable behaviors in a parent simultaneously.

Do some of these behaviors combined with alcoholism affect adult children differently to increase or lessen the impact of parental alcoholism? In Table 2.2 the different types of behaviors found in alcoholic parents are compared to the percentage of adult children who felt that they were highly affected by the alcoholism. The table shows that adult children were not only affected by the alcoholism, but also that the type of behavior displayed by the alcoholic parent contributed to how significantly they felt they were affected. Alcoholism coupled with offensive behavior was found to affect adult children the most, even though as indicated on Table 2.1, verbal belligerency was the most commonly associated behavior. The next highest was found among adult children with verbally

Table 2.2

Behavior of Alcoholic Parents and the Degree of Effect on the Lives of Adult Children of Alcoholics

Alcoholic's Behavior When Drinking	Degree of Effect		
	Low	Moderate	High
Offensive	3.8%	7.7%	88.5%
Verbally Belligerent	6.5	9.3	84.2
Passive	12.2	12.2	75.6
Carefree	22.1	4.4	73.5
Other	20.8	9.7	69.5

belligerent alcoholic parents, followed by passive and other types of behaviors.

The key to surviving an alcoholic family is the ability to adapt to the situation. The adult child may be able to remember many times when he or she was quiet, kept things to himself or herself, making sure the alcoholic did not have access to information. Depending upon the mood or behavior of the alcoholic parent, the child responded accordingly, but perhaps inconsistently.

For example, the alcoholic parent engages in inconsistent role behavior by fulfilling the roles in at least four ways. He or she plays one role when sober, and another when drunk. A third role is played when the alcoholic becomes anxious or agitated, usually before drinking. The fourth occurs when the alcoholic is having a hangover and feels guilty or remorseful.

A typical scenario could be that on Friday night and Saturday, all hell is breaking loose. Sunday is hangover day, and Monday is full of guilt and remorse. Tuesday and Wednesday are fairly calm. Thursday begins with anxiety and agitation, which leads to drinking on Friday, with the cycle beginning again.

Just imagine yourself as a child in this family who wants to ask for something. Like most children, you hope you can get what you want. What day of the week would you ask? Some may ask on Tuesday or Wednesday because this would appear to be the most normal time to ask. However, many adult children remember asking on particular days when they felt that the probability of compliance was the greatest. Therefore, some would pick hangover or guilt days, while others would ask when the alcoholic was drinking.

I remember a woman in New York telling me "I always asked my father when he was drunk because then he would give me whatever I wanted." After a while the adult child learned that the probability of the pay-off was more important than the health of the request. However, the adult child may remember that he or she also felt guilty or remorseful, because he or she was using the guilt or remorse of the alcoholic to get what he or she wanted.

Additionally, the adult child may have felt angry or resentful that he or she had to "manipulate" the situation to get what he or she wanted, rather than being able to ask any day of the week. Thus the child is drawn into the manipulation game also and experiences inconsistency personally, as well as on the parental level.

This manipulation of each other becomes evident when one looks at other issues associated with the type or kind of alcoholic that the adult child experienced. Alcoholic parents who were extremely passive and spent much of their time sleeping or drinking away from home may have affected their child one way, whereas alcoholics who were verbally belligerent may have affected their child in entirely different ways.

Another type of alcoholic parent is the parent who treats everything in life as a joke. The alcoholic makes light of everything and accuses everyone else of being too serious. This could have been stressful for the adult child while growing up because he or she could never count on the alcoholic for serious responses, support or adequate parental advice.

Additionally there is the alcoholic parent who became aggressive and engaged in family violence, thus placing the adult child in the position of "double jeopardy". Not only did adult children with an abusive parent experience parental alcoholism, but also they were subjected to child abuse, sexual abuse or as witnesses to spouse abuse.

Parents who were binge drinkers may have had different effects on the adult child than parents who depended upon daily intake of alcohol. There are also parents who, although alcoholic, did not bring out extreme negative feelings in their children because the adult child perceived that he or she was still loved in spite of the alcoholism. Just as different parenting styles affect children differently, so do different types of alcoholics and their behaviors or personalities affect their children differently.

The adult child may remember that when the parent was drunk he or she acted a certain way, but when the parent was sober he or she could be more himself/herself. When the alcoholic parent was agitated, however, the adult child may remember being very careful to stay well out of their way.

I once heard Jael Greenleaf address an audience of adult children of alcoholics in Los Angeles and say that she believed that most adult children considered themselves to be clairvoyant (Greenleaf, 1983). I remember thinking to myself "That isn't true, but I knew you were going to say that." It may not be clairvoyance, but consider it this way. Perhaps as a young child the adult child began to learn the relationship between cause and effect in observing other people. The survival of the child is often dependent upon being able to anticipate adult's moods or behaviors, particularly in different situations. Consequently, one reason that adult children of alcoholics have not been affected the same may be that the differences in personality and behaviors found in alcoholic parents are neither the same nor consistent.

3. Different Reactions to Stress

Families under stress produce children under stress, but not all children react to stress the same way. Some adult children learned to handle stress well and can still handle it. Other adult children have difficulty coping, and much of their current stress reminds them of their childhood. Although it is true that stress may produce many negative characteristics in children, it is also true that children may be able to develop prosocial behaviors to handle it, and thus are not as negatively affected. It may be possible to learn just as much from adult children who have developed high levels of resilience to stress as it is to learn from those adult children who break down under stress. By examining stress and childhood, it is possible to study how children in dysfunctional families learn to handle and adapt to stress. How the adult child learned to handle the stress of the alcoholic family may reveal clues as to how they handle stress today.

According to Avis Brenner (1984), children who are vulnerable to the negative aspects of stress, develop characteristics such as:

1. Overly sensitive and shy
2. Moody, irritable
3. Lonely, not able to make friends easily
4. Easily angered
5. Constantly complaining

Children who are extremely vulnerable to stress display these characteristics:

1. Withdrawn and preoccupied
2. Frequently sick without organic cause
3. Secretive, non-communicative
4. Belligerent
5. Prone to frequent nightmares

Obviously, not all children who are affected negatively by stress will possess all of the characteristics, but the adult child may be able to look back and identify with some of these behaviors as his or her way of handling stress. Even if you identified with some of these, however, you may feel that you had other ways of handling stress and that these were not as negative. This may be due to the fact that you were able to develop prosocial or resilient types of behaviors to handle stress.

For example, James Anthony describes the characteristics of children who have high levels of invulnerability to stress (Anthony, 1984). These behaviors include:

1. Children who know how to attract and use the support of adults
2. Children who actively try to master their own environment and have a sense of their own power; often they volunteer to help others
3. Children who develop a high degree of autonomy early in life
4. Children who get involved in various activities or projects and do well in most things that they do
5. Children who are socially at ease and who make others feel comfortable around them

Like most survivors of stress, you probably possess a combination of the above patterns of adapting to stress. Your particular combination probably depends upon which patterns of coping behaviors you developed to handle the situation. Patterns of coping have positive and negative outcomes which depend upon whether they were long- or short-term patterns. Generally, the longer the pattern, the higher the probability that it became negative. This is particularly true for the adult child who has carried his or her negative adaptive patterns from childhood stress into adulthood, without adjusting or abandoning the negative aspects of the patterns.

How can patterns of coping with stress have both positive and negative aspects? It depends on the coping behavior and the degree to which the behavior is used to handle stress. Four common ways for children to handle stress are: denial, regression, withdrawal, and impulsive acting out.

Denial is often interpreted in alcoholic homes as a barrier to treatment. It may enable the child to survive the parental alcoholism. For the child in a crisis, however, denial actually may be functional. For example, the child may deny that the problem exists at times, in order to alleviate the emotional pain or to take time out from thinking about the situation. All children in stress need an "emotional vacation" from the stress in order to survive. Denial is one way to create this "time out". Additionally, denial may be a way for the child to try to maintain a balance in his/her life. These aspects of denial for the child in stress thus become a pattern to help to handle the stress. Obviously, the negative side of denial occurs when it is carried to the point that no intervention is allowed since no problem exists.

Regression is used by many children in stress as an attempt to return to a more secure state. For many children, small doses of regression may have resulted in their being comforted by adults around them, thus the regressive behavior of the child was reinforced. The negative side of this develops when the child becomes too demanding for attention and unfortunately develops an unhealthy sense of dependence, thus regressing to a point where he or she cannot or will not care for him or herself.

Withdrawal, the third way of handling stress, can be used by children in crisis as a way of physically or emotionally removing themselves from the situation and focusing attention elsewhere. This may provide relief for the child but can become complicated if the withdrawal leads to isolation and a lack of contact with support systems.

"**Acting out**" is used by some children of alcoholics, as well as other children in crisis situations. Although this may seem inappropriate, it may be a way for children under stress to draw attention to themselves instead of considering the real problems (i.e., the alcoholic parent). If carried to extremes, this pattern of coping becomes a self-destructive pattern.

There are many other ways in which children under stress develop coping patterns. Perhaps you engaged in some of the above behaviors, or had other patterns which you still use in adulthood. Some could be the use of humor, helping others and the ability to anticipate stressful situations.

Research has shown that adults who have a healthy sense of humor are more capable of handling stress well. This was also found to be true in young children. Rather than cry, you may have used sarcasm, jokes and humor to alleviate the seriousness of stressful situations.

Many adult children have become exceptionally adept at helping others. Have you ever wondered where the helping professions would be today without adult children of alcoholics? Forgetting your own problems by helping others may be a positive way to handle stress, as long as you do not forget yourself in the process. Helping others can provide a healthy and much needed sense of purpose, satisfaction and self-esteem for many adults. It helps to provide a sense of being needed and of accomplishment.

Finally, many adult children may have handled stress better than others because they learned to be able to anticipate potentially stressful situations. They were able to foresee and plan accordingly, thus being better able to prepare to protect themselves. Were you the kind of adult child who could almost predict when the house would be emotionally disrupted? If so, you may have been better prepared to handle the stress than adult children who were continually caught unprepared.

All of these different responses to stress produce different outcomes. Those who had the greatest repertoire for handling stress are probably those adults who still handle stress well today. The Peter Principle states that the greatest part of courage is having done the thing before (Peters, 1970).

Although none of us likes negative situations, some of us can handle them better than others. Additionally, not all adults consider all stresses to be negative. It is commonly agreed in research that some adults function better under an optimal degree of stress, whereas others have difficulty handling even minimal stresses in their lives. Certainly, living with an alcoholic parent was a major stress for adult children of alcoholics. Not only how this stress was handled but also the many different responses created explain why adult children are not all affected the same way by having grown up in the alcoholic home.

4. Perception

As an adult child of an alcoholic, the most critical variable that accounts for why you may have been affected differently is your perception of the situation while growing up. Families of alcoholics not only share different perceptions of the situation, but also individuals in the same family will have different perceptions of the same experience.

Perceptions and reality are not always the same. Whatever you perceive as real, you react to accordingly. If you perceived that you were in a totally hopeless situation while growing up, you probably reacted hopelessly. If you perceived that you had some control over the situation or that you were not alone, you may have perceived the situation as negative but not hopeless. Some adult children definitely feel that they were reared in extreme crisis situations, whereas others perceived that the crisis was manageable. Additionally, your perception not only of the situation but also of the degree to which you feel you were emotionally affected must be considered.

Table 2.3 illustrates the differences among adult children of alcoholics regarding their perceptions of the degree to which they feel they were emotionally affected by parental alcoholism.

Table 2.3

Adult Children of Alcoholics' Perceptions of the Effects of Parental Alcoholism on Their Lives

Degree Affected	Percent of ACoA's (n=504)
Highly affected	78.2%
Moderately affected	11.1
Not affected	10.7

As indicated on Table 2.3 the majority of adult children felt that they were highly affected, but almost one in four indicated that they were not. These different perceptions may have resulted from two considerations.

The first is the degree of power that you felt over the situation relative to handling the negative implications, and the second is the degree to which you perceived that you had access to some help in resolving some of the problems. What often makes a crisis a crisis is not just the situation itself but whether or not the situation can be resolved or managed by you or others. Obviously, a crisis situation that is manageable is perceived as less detrimental than one over which you have no control.

Lee Ann Hoff, in her book, *People in Crisis,* explains that a crisis develops in four phases (Hoff, 1984). In phase one the individual is exposed to a traumatic event and tries to use familiar problem-solving mechanisms to reduce or eliminate anxiety and concern. In phase two the individual's usual problem-solving abilities fail and thus anxiety and tension increase. Phase three begins when the person tries to use every available resource to solve the situation, but it remains unresolved and the anxiety increases further. This is especially true for the many families who isolate themselves because of alcoholism and thus unknowingly reduce the amount of available outside resources to help. Phase four is when the person is in the crisis state. At this point internal strengths and social support are lacking, the problems remain unresolved and the tension and anxiety reach an unbearable degree (Hoff, 1984).

Adult children obviously were raised not only in a crisis situation, but also in a crisis of exceptional duration. Unlike the individual who experiences a short-term traumatic event, the adult child was continually exposed. During this time the adult child began to perceive not only the situation, but also how he or she should react to the situation. I do not think that adult children of alcoholics planned their reactions, but rather did what seemed to make the most sense at the time. Besides, they may have perceived that they had little choice.

Many of the different patterns of reactions by adult children may have been based on the degree of power the adult child felt was available to control the situation. For most children of alcoholics, however, the sense of powerlessness over the situation further complicated having an alcoholic parent.

While growing up, the adult child was powerless over at least three problems. First, the adult child was powerless to stop the alcoholic from drinking. Second, the adult child was powerless over the relationship between the parents as spouses. We know from research that the negative relationship between the parents is considered more detrimental than the drinking by the majority of children of alcoholics (Cork, 1969). Third, the adult child was powerless to leave while growing up. Many adult children initially saw their solution to the crisis as just a matter of leaving, only to find that while they may have physically removed themselves from the source of the crisis, many of the emotional issues remain unresolved. The initial idea was, "All I have to do is leave and I will not only leave all of this behind, but also my life will automatically improve." However, many adult children left and were surprised they did not have the psychological understanding to improve their emotional lives.

Much of this could stem from the possible outcomes of a crisis, which again explains why not all adult children are affected the same.

Hoff (1984) states that three outcomes can happen to a person from a crisis. First, the person reduces the intolerable tension and anxiety by developing patterns of negative behaviors. These may range from becoming isolated, withdrawn or depressed to exaggerating the impact and blaming others for your misfortune, or to turning to self-destructive behaviors, ranging from addiction to suicide.

Second, the individual can return to a pre-crisis state. This is possible by using one's internal strengths and social support networks to manage the crisis effectively. However, this outcome does not imply that new emotional growth has resulted from the experience, but instead the person manages to return to his or her normal state of mind.

Third, the person not only finds the problem manageable personally or with the help of others, but the person grows from the experience and uses the new problem-solving skills for greater personal strength. It is possible that adult children may be found in all three of the categories, depending upon their perceptions and their reactions to the perceptions in different patterns.

The problems of inconsistency in the alcoholic family, however, further complicate perception. For many adult children it was difficult to get an adequate and consistent perception of what was happening in their family. It is one thing to experience a crisis, and yet another to be in one that is highly inconsistent.

Judy Seixas and Geraldine Youcha refer to the alcoholic family as the "disorderly-orderly" family (Seixas, 1985). On one hand, the adult child remembers living in chaos and on the other, remembers trying to convince himself or herself that it was manageable or an "orderly" chaos.

It is difficult to get an accurate perception of a situation which is characterized by mixed messages. The adult child may remember such statements as, "I love you; go away and leave me alone" or "There is nothing wrong, but don't tell anyone" or "I'm fine; call them up and tell them I'm sick." These mixed messages contribute to the difficulty of developing an accurate perception. However, some children of alcoholics were able to develop perceptions of the situation that were not as detrimental to them later as an adult child. Those who developed less problematic perceptions may have been able to perceive that they were separate from the alcoholism, that they had a sense of power over themselves, that others were willing to help with the situation, or that their perceptions and the reality were synonymous and they were able to adjust more consistently and appropriately to parental alcoholism.

5. Gender

Are adult children of alcoholic mothers affected differently than adult children of alcoholic fathers? Do daughters of alcoholic mothers perceive the impact of parental alcoholism the same as sons? Do sons of alcoholic fathers experience the same emotional implications as daughters? What about the perceptions of sons and daughters of two alcoholic parents? It is obvious that there are many possible gender combinations that need to be considered when assessing why adult children are not all affected the same way. To date there has been little research on possible gender implications and differences of effects.

Initially, there are several issues that need to be considered. One issue is related to how each gender fulfills his or her role as parent. Another is how each gender fulfills his or her role as an alcoholic parent. Are women or men more affected by alcoholism when it comes to being an effective parent? This side of the issue addresses the gender of the parent, but what about the gender of the adult child? It is possible that many of the generalizations about personality characteristics do not apply if the gender of the adult child is considered.

Daughters of alcoholics may be affected differently than sons. The tables in this section contain charts of the most commonly agreed upon clinical observations of personality characteristics. These tables are concerned with the gender of the alcoholic and the gender of the adult child. The findings in these tables indicate that there are many similarities between sons and daughters of alcoholics, but differences of degree of effects and areas affected are also indicated. Additionally, it appears that the gender of the alcoholic parent or that having two alcoholic parents has different implications for sons and daughters.

Initially, however, it is helpful to compare the responses of adult children of alcoholics with those of adult sons and daughters of non-alcoholic parents. In Table 2.4 these comparisons are made. Sons and daughters of non-alcoholic parents scored almost identically, and there was almost an even split between which gender was more likely to identify with which characteristic. In fact, on four of the characteristics the scores were even, men scored higher on six items, and women scored higher on ten items. Additionally, the differences in scores on any individual item were small. However, when comparing these scores to adult children of alcoholics, obvious differences become apparent. Besides the obvious difference that adult children scored higher than the control group, the differences between sons and daughters start to develop.

For example, daughters of alcoholics had higher total scores on identifying with the personality characteristics. Additionally, the evenness between the two genders on (half identifying with some characteristics and half identifying with others) begins to disappear. When parental alcoholism is considered, daughters now have higher scores on nineteen of the twenty items. Thus Table 2.4 not only reflects the similarity and differences between adults with alcoholic parents and those without, but also raises the question of what accounts for these differences and under what parental gender differences are they most likely to increase or decrease.

Table 2.4

Personality Characteristics of Adult Sons and Daughters of Alcoholic and Non-Alcoholic Parents by Gender

	(Alcoholic Par)		(Non-Alcoholic)	
	Daughters	Sons	Daughters	Sons
1. I guess at what is normal	3.19	3.04	2.51	2.51
2. I have difficulty following projects thought to completion.	2.86	2.65	2.41	2.43
3. I lie when it would be just as easy to tell the truth.	2.18	2.23	1.81	1.81
4. I judge myself without mercy.	3.610	3.37	2.96	2.81
5. I have difficulty having fun.	3.13	3.06	2.37	2.50
6. I take myself very seriously.	3.92	3.65	3.40	3.40
7. I have difficulty with intimate relationships	3.54	3.36	2.74	2.72
8. I overreact to changes over which I have no control.	3.42	3.16	2.83	2.73
9. I feel different from other people.	3.24	3.16	2.76	2.71
10. I constantly seek approval and affirmation.	3.48	3.37	3.01	2.96
11. I am either super responsible or irresponsible	3.42	3.40	2.74	2.60
12. I am extremely loyal even in the face of evidence that the loyalty is undeserved.	3.41	3.21	3.04	3.03
13. I look for immediate as opposed to deferred gratification.	3.09	3.07	2.67	2.70
14. I lock myself into a course of action without serious consideration to alternate choices or consequences.	2.79	2.67	2.32	2.67
15. I seek tension and crisis and then complain.	2.65	2.40	2.12	2.05
16. I avoid conflict or aggravate it; but rarely deal with it.	2.83	2.77	2.42	2.42
17. I fear rejection and abandonment, yet I reject others.				
18. I fear failure, but have difficulty handling success.	3.42	3.31	2.77	2.75
19. I fear criticism and judgment, yet I criticize others.	3.19	3.07	2.68	2.66
20. I manage my time poorly and do not set my priorities in a way that works well for me.	2.90	2.74	2.54	2.74
TOTALS	63.37	60.54	52.45	52.07

Score 5 = Always, 4 = Often, 3 = Sometimes, 2 = Seldom, 1 = Never

Alcoholic Mothers

Of the adult children of alcoholics in the national study, approximately 20% had an alcoholic mother. Although it is true that we do not know how many women alcoholics there are in our society, it does not appear that there are as many as male alcoholics. Although adult children of alcoholics may feel unique or different from others, those with alcoholic mothers may feel even more isolated because of several factors.

1. Having an alcoholic mother is not as common as an alcoholic father.

2. Only one out of ten males will stay with an alcoholic female, compared with the nine out of ten women who will stay with an alcoholic male, thus greatly increasing the probability of single parenting for alcoholic women who are able to maintain child custody.

3. Societal implications for alcoholism in females may be different than for males because of greater stigmatization and the "fallen angel" syndrome of blaming the victim more in the case of women alcoholics.

4. There is the issue of the impact on children and child development when the mother is the alcoholic as opposed to the father. These considerations may make the adult child of an alcoholic mother consider himself or herself even more unique than adult children in general.

However, we must not only consider the gender of the parent, but also the gender of the child. Table 2.5 contains the differences in scores on personality characteristics of sons and daughters of alcoholic mothers. Thus the question is, are sons and daughters affected in the same areas and to the same degrees, or is the effect of having an alcoholic mother different for daughters than for sons?

It appears on Table 2.5 that sons of alcoholic mothers have a greater degree of the personality characterisitics identified with adult children of alcoholics. Although there are many similarities in scores between sons and daughters on Table 2.5, there are

Table 2.5

Personality Characteristics of Adult Sons and Daughters of Alcoholic Mothers

	Daughters	Sons
1. I guess at what is normal.	3.28	3.10
2. I have difficulty following projects through to completion.	2.84	2.50
3. I lie when it would be just as easy to tell the truth.	2.03	2.40
4. I judge myself without mercy.	3.42	3.25
5. I have difficulty having fun.	3.10	3.25
6. I take myself very seriously.	3.97	3.65
7. I have difficulty with intimate relationships.	3.45	3.75
8. I overreact to changes over which I have no control.	3.55	3.25
9. I feel different from other people	3.27	3.30
10. I constantly seek approval and affirmation.	3.39	3.90
11. I am either super responsible or irresponsible.	3.42	3.85
12. I am extremely loyal even in the face of evidence that the loyalty is undeserved.	3.71	3.30
13. I look for immediate as opposed to deferred gratification.	3.00	3.30
14. I lock myself into a course of action without serious consideration to alternate choices or consequences.	2.74	2.60
15. I seek tension and crisis and then complain.	2.50	2.45
16. I avoid conflict or aggravate it, but rarely deal with it.	2.67	3.25
17. I fear rejection and abandonment, yet I reject others.	2.68	3.20
18. I fear failure, but have difficulty handing success.	3.13	3.35
19. I fear criticism and judgment, yet I criticize others.	2.87	3.50
20. I manage my time poorly and do not set my priorities in a way that works well for me.	2.74	2.60
TOTALS	61.76	63.75

Score   5 = Always, 4 = Often, 3 = Sometimes, 2 = Seldom, 1 = Never

some interesting differences. For example, the top three scores for daughters of alcoholic mothers were in the following areas:

Taking yourself very seriously
Being extremely loyal
Overreacting to change

However, sons of alcoholic mothers rated three different issues as their top characteristics. These were:

Constantly seeking affirmation and approval
Being either super responsible or irresponsible
Having difficulty with intimate relationships

Additionally, it is interesting to note the three areas where sons and daughters differ the most on their scores on personality characteristics. These differences were most notable in the areas of:

Fear of criticism and judgment
Seeking approval and affirmation
Avoiding conflict or aggravating it, but rarely dealing with it

Although the overall degree of differences are not great, sons and daughters appear to be affected not only in different areas but also to different degrees when exposed to maternal alcoholism. Sons of alcoholic mothers scored higher than daughters on eleven of the twenty characteristics. It is probable, therefore, that adult sons of alcoholic mothers have different issues to resolve than do daughters and the degree of resolution needed also will differ.

Alcoholic Fathers

It is much more common to have an alcoholic father in our society than an alcoholic mother. In this study approximately 60% of the adult children had an alcoholic father only. This statistic is in agreement with other studies. Although it may be more common, does having an alcoholic father have the same degree of effects on adult children as having an alcoholic mother? Do sons and daughters interpret the experience similarly? Table 2.6 contains the scores on personality characteristics of sons and daughters of alcoholic fathers.

Although the personality characteristics are similar for both sons and daughters, one of the major differences is the areas that concern each the most. For daughters of alcoholic fathers, the highest three personality characteristics were concerned with:

Taking herself very seriously
Judging herself without mercy
Constantly seeking affirmation and approval

It is interesting to note that when the mother was alcoholic, adult sons and daughters had different areas of concerns. Sons of alcoholic fathers, on the other hand, had the same top three concerns as daughters of alcoholic fathers but to different

Table 2.6

Personality Characteristics of Adult Sons and Daughters of Alcoholics Fathers

	Daughters	Sons
1. I guess at what is normal.	3.15	3.01
2. I have difficulty following projects through to completion.	2.87	2.64
3. I lie when it would be just as easy to tell the truth.	2.20	2.18
4. I judge myself without mercy.	3.59	3.36
5. I have difficulty having fun.	3.10	2.99
6. I take myself very seriously.	3.90	3.64
7. I have difficulty with intimate relationships.	3.50	3.28
8. I overreact to changes over which I have no control.	3.46	3.11
9. I feel different from other people	3.24	3.07
10. I constantly seek approval and affirmation.	3.51	3.28
11. I am either super responsible or irresponsible.	3.36	3.28
12. I am extremely loyal even in the face of evidence that the loyalty is undeserved.	3.34	3.25
13. I look for immediate as opposed to deferred gratification.	3.16	3.01
14. I lock myself into a course of action without serious consideration to alternate choices or consequences.	2.76	2.64
15. I seek tension and crisis and then complain.	2.62	2.36
16. I avoid conflict or aggravate it, but rarely deal with it.	2.85	2.66
17. I fear rejection and abandonment, yet I reject others.	3.22	2.75
18. I fear failure, but have difficulty handing success.	3.48	3.28
19. I fear criticism and judgment, yet I criticize others.	3.32	2.95
20. I manage my time poorly and do not set my priorities in a way that works well for me.	2.88	2.78
TOTALS	63.51	59.52

Score 5 = Always, 4 = Often, 3 = Sometimes, 2 = Seldom, 1 = Never

degrees (items scores were carried to the .000 level to determine differences). Thus, for sons of alcoholic fathers the top three areas of concern were:

Taking himself very seriously
Judging himself without mercy
Constantly seeking approval and affirmation

The greatest differences for sons and daughters occurred in these areas:

Fear of rejection and abandonment
Fear of criticism and judgment
Overreacting to changes over which one has no control

Again, as was the case with having an alcoholic mother, sons and daughters appear to be affected differently, but to a lesser degree of variation in the ranking of personality characteristics. What is strikingly different in the case of the alcoholic father is that daughters scored higher on all twenty personality characteristics than sons. This was not the case of the alcoholic mother, where the son scored higher on eleven of the characteristics. This finding does raise interesting speculation and implications for cross-gender alcoholism, in which the alcoholic is the opposite gender of the adult child.

Both of these cases, however, have one thing in common for both sons and daughters, and that is that only one of the parents was alcoholic. What about the effects on sons and daughters who grew up with two alcoholic parents?

Two Alcoholic Parents

In approximately 20% of the cases in this study, adult children of alcoholics had two alcoholic parents. Research indicates that where both parents are alcoholic the alcoholism developed at earlier ages for both parents, thus increasing the probability that children of alcoholics were exposed to parental alcoholism at earlier ages themselves than when only one parent is alcoholic (Goodwin, 1984).

Additionally, other research suggests that adult children of two alcoholic parents are more likely to begin drinking themselves at earlier ages and that they are themselves more susceptible to alcoholism at earlier ages (Volicer, 1983). Where both parents are alcoholic, there may be a variety of other associated issues that compound parental alcoholism for children. For example, there is not the presence of the nonalcoholic spouse to fill in as parent as an offsetting factor.

The children may be faced with both emotional and physical neglect, which may lead to a higher probability of foster placement than in families with one alcoholic parent. Table 2.7 contains the responses of sons and daughters of two alcoholic parents.

Indicated in Table 2.7 is that daughters of two alcoholic parents appear to be more affected than sons. Both sons and daughters share two out of three of their top areas of concerns,

Table 2.7

Characteristics of Adult Sons and Daughters of Two Alcoholic Parents

	Daughters	Sons
1. I guess at what is normal.	3.27	3.07
2. I have difficulty following projects through to completion.	2.86	2.69
3. I lie when it would be just as easy to tell the truth.	2.20	2.31
4. I judge myself without mercy.	3.74	3.44
5. I have difficulty having fun.	3.21	3.16
6. I take myself very seriously.	3.96	3.64
7. I have difficulty with intimate relationships.	3.72	3.51
8. I overreact to changes over which I have no control.	3.32	3.24
9. I feel different from other people	3.22	3.36
10. I constantly seek approval and affirmation.	3.48	3.38
11. I am either super responsible or irresponsible.	3.56	3.50
12. I am extremely loyal even in the face of evidence that the loyalty is undeserved.	3.49	3.00
13. I look for immediate as opposed to deferred gratification.	3.00	3.09
14. I lock myself into a course of action without serious consideration to alternate choices or consequences.	2.90	2.80
15. I seek tension and crisis and then complain.	2.80	2.53
16. I avoid conflict or aggravate it, but rarely deal with it.	2.85	2.93
17. I fear rejection and abandonment, yet I reject others.	3.09	3.02
18. I fear failure, but have difficulty handing success.	3.43	3.33
19. I fear criticism and judgment, yet I criticize others.	3.01	3.24
20. I manage my time poorly and do not set my priorities in a way that works well for me.	2.96	2.76
TOTALS	64.07	62.00

Score 5 = Always, 4 = Often, 3 = Sometimes, 2 = Seldom, 1 = Never

but again the degree of impact is different. For daughters of two alcoholic parents, their top three characterisitcs were:

Taking herself very seriously
Judging herself without mercy
Having difficulty with intimate relationships

Sons of two alcoholic parents ranked the following characteristics the highest:

Taking himself very seriously
Having difficulty with intimate relationships
Being super responsible or irresponsible

The greatest differences in scores of characteristics between sons and daughters of two alcoholic parents occurred in the areas of:

Being extremely loyal
Taking themselves very seriously
Judging themselves without mercy

The variable of gender appears to have a significant impact on the issues that are identified for sons and daughters of alcoholics. It is difficult, however, to distinguish the exact relationship of gender implications. That is, is it the gender of the parent that makes a difference, the gender of the adult child or a combination of the interaction of both genders? Additionally, one could examine the master status roles that parents play in their childrens' lives. For example, is it more critical to impair the performance of one of the parental roles than the other? Another factor might be how the child fulfills his or her own role when one of the parental roles is impaired. If mother is alcoholic, this obviously affects her performance as a parent, but how does her role impairment cause changes in the child's role? Are children of alcoholics more capable of adjusting and handling the impairment of one parental role better than the other?

Another gender consideration is how does the alcoholism in one parent affect the ability of the other parent to fulfill his or her parental responsiblities? For example, the first variable discussed in this chapter asked how the degree of alcoholism in the alcoholic parent affects the ability of the parent to fulfill his or her role as parent. However, what about how well the non-alcoholic parent fulfills his or her role? This may be a gender issue as well.

If the mother is alcoholic, this obviously affects her role, but how does it also affect the ability of her husband to be an effective parent? In a study by Carol Williams (1983), this issue was considered. She studied approximately 100 families and was concerned with the effects on the quality of child care, depending on which parent was the alcoholic. Williams examined the gender of the alcoholic parent and effects on children by examining the quality of child care, the level of family stability, incidence of any child abuse and child neglect.

Table 2.8 illustrates her findings. In the table all rankings are shown as high, middle or low to illustrate the differences in rank

Table 2.8

Gender of Alcoholic Parent and the Quality of Child Care

	Quality of Child Care	Family Stability	Child Abuse	Neglect
Both Parents	low	middle	high	middle
Mother Only	middle	low	middle	high
Father Only	high	high	low	low

between the effects of an alcoholic father only, and alcoholic mother only, or two alcoholic parents.

This study demonstrates again the different influences that gender of alcoholic parent can have on children. It also raises some interesting issues. In the above case of two alcoholic parents, we see that the quality of child care was the lowest and that the level of child abuse was the highest. This would agree with other research that indicates that if both parents are alcoholic, the alcoholism was likely to develop at earlier ages and that younger parents are more likely to abuse children physically than are older parents (Strauss 1980).

The findings on alcoholic mothers only show that this causes the lowest levels of family stability. However, we know that very few husbands will stay with an alcoholic wife and thus contributes to this problem by leaving.

For fathers only, however, many of the issues appear not to be as devastating. This effect was also found among the adult children indicated on the earlier tables where having an alcoholic father produced lower scores by the adult children on the personality items. Is this due to the fact that alcoholism in fathers is not as critical for children or is it due to other factors? Again, the answer may be that it is a gender issue, particularly because we are concerned with the quality of child care, and we know that in the cases of male alcoholism, the majority of women will stay. Thus it may be that the wife is directly or indirectly fulfilling many of the parenting responsibilities and reducing the impact of his drinking in certain areas for the children.

An interesting question to consider might be is it possible that women can tolerate alcoholism better in their husbands and still fulfill their roles as parents than men can tolerate alcoholism in their wives and still fulfill their roles as parents? The issue of gender is a highly interactive variable with a diversity of outcomes for adult children of alcoholics.

From this discussion and presentation of the national data, what gender combinations are the most devastating for adult daughters and adult sons? Using the total scores on the different personality characteristics, it appears that for daughters of alcoholics, having two alcoholic parents has the greatest impact, followed by having an alcoholic father, and least by having an alcoholic mother. For sons of alcoholic parents, the greatest impact occurred when he had an alcoholic mother. Next was having two alcoholic parents, and the least impact on sons was that of having an alcoholic father. It is interesting to note that both adult sons and daughters scored lowest on the personality characteristics when their alcoholic parent was of the same gender. It should be noted, however, that the range of scores for each of the gender combinations was not that great, but the degree and the differences in which personality characteristics were most identified was important. For example, daughters of alcoholic mothers may have diffferent issues to work on in recovery than if they had an alcoholic father or both parents alcoholic. Sons of alcoholics also have different issues they will bring to recovery. Additionally, it is obvious that both sons and daughters of alcoholic parents of either gender will have much in common with the powerful issues of self-criticism, taking yourself too seriously, needing approval, being extremely loyal and most important, having difficulty with intimate relationships dominating the recovery process.

6. Age

Age can affect the outcome of exposure to parental alcoholism in a variety of ways. One is how old the child was when parental alcoholism developed. If you were born into an alcoholic home, it would be different than if your parent became alcoholic when you were five or fifteen. Thus it is not only the exposure to alcoholism that is significant, but also *when* the exposure for the adult child began.

Additionally, it is doubtful that the child was aware of alcoholism as the problem in his or her home, but rather realized that he or she lived in a house that was "different". Being exposed to alcoholism and understanding alcoholism may be two different things, the understanding being related to age. A young child may be able to understand the physical effects of getting drunk long before he or she can understand the dynamics of alcoholism and its impact on the family, particularly on family relationships.

Age becomes an important factor when we consider the adult child from a developmental perspective. That is, what is the effect of parental alcoholism at different ages on children? Additionally, a developmental approach would consider what are the normal developmental issues that are occurring for the child at that age and how are these normal problems compounded by exposure to parental alcoholism.

According to Erikson and his developmental levels, some of the normal issues for young children to resolve focus on the development of trust, of a sense of autonomy, of initiative, and of a sense of accomplishment (Erikson, 1963). Besides working through these normal childhood issues, the young child of the alcoholic will face the additional ones arising from having an alcoholic parent.

For example, if your parent became alcoholic when you were eight, you were far more likely to be concerned with your physical safety, with fear of abandonment and with parental arguments than you were with the drinking.

In her work with young children of alcoholics, Ellen Morehouse identifies seven major areas of concerns that affect children at this age who have an alcoholic parent (Morehouse, 1982). These concerns are:

1. Worrying about the health of the alcoholic parent.
2. Being upset and angry by the unpredictable and inconsistent behavior of the alcoholic parent and the lack of support from the non-alcoholic parent.
3. Worrying about fights and arguments between their parents.
4. Being scared and upset by the violence or the possibility of violence in their family.
5. Being upset by the parent's inappropriate behavior, which can include criminal or sexual behavior.
6. Being disappointed by broken promises and by feeling unloved.
7. Feeling responsible for their parent's drinking.

How many of these feelings do you as an adult have now? How did exposure to these issues affect your childhood? How has your childhood affected your adulthood? Adult children who were not exposed to parental alcoholism during their early childhood may have different perceptions of the experience as well as of their childhood. How you handled these issues then may affect you now.

What about your adolescence and parental alcoholism? This developmental age is argued by many to be the most critical for it is concerned not only with identity formation, but also with issues of sexuality and the development of the ability to achieve positive emotional intimacy in our lives. By the time some people become adolescents, they already will have experienced parental alcoholism if it started during their childhood, while for others the alcoholism developed during their adolescence.

The major areas of concern for adolescent children of alcoholics are (Ackerman, 1986):

1. Concerned about their own substance use and if alcoholism is hereditary.
2. Concerned about the health of or how to get their alcoholic parent to stop drinking.
3. How to survive their parents' troubled relationship.
4. Concerned about their family's alcoholism and its effects on their friendships, dating and "reputation".
5. How to live with an alcoholic.
6. How to develop better survival skills for coping and getting help.
7. Concerned about other issues that may be related, such as physical abuse, incest or how and why they may be affected by alcoholism.

Which of these concerns remain with you today? Although you may have experienced exposure to parental alcoholism years ago, your age at the time of exposure may still have a profound effect on you today. During your adolescence you were confronted with the normal issues of establishing your identity, formulating your sexuality and preparing yourself for achieving intimacy at the same time. As a child of an alcoholic, however, you may have had the additional issues mentioned above impacting on you. Many unresolved issues in adolescence are carried over into adulthood, and the adult child may find himself or herself unable to confront the unresolved issues and are thereby trapped in "perpetual adolescence" in certain areas of their lives.

Another factor is not only at what age you first were exposed, but also how old you were when you were willing to acknowledge that one or both of your parents had a drinking problem. In the national study it was interesting to note that not only did adult children acknowledge the status of an alcoholic parent at different ages, but also that the gender of the alcoholic parent influenced when they ackowledged it.

Table 2.9 contains the different ages of adult children when they first acknowledged that one or both parents had a drinking problem.

Table 2.9

Age of Adult Children of Alcoholics When Parental Alcoholism was Acknowledged

Alcoholic Parent	Average Age
Both Parents	14.3 years
Father only	12.7
Mother only	18.4

As indicated in Table 2.9 the ages of acknowledgment differed depending upon the gender of the alcoholic. Between alcoholic mothers and alcoholic fathers, there appears to be a notable difference in the age at which acknowledgment by the adult child occurred. It is obvious that this situation is more than just an age factor and that it is closely related to the previous discussions on gender implications. The later recognition for alcoholism in mothers may be caused by several factors.

Some research indicates that women develop alcoholism later in life than men, therefore their ages and the ages of their children would be higher (Wilsnack, 1984). Second, having an alcoholic mother as opposed to an alcoholic father may be harder for some children to accept. Finally, alcoholism in women is not as readily accepted in society as in men and therefore the denial process can be even longer in the case of maternal alcoholism.

This elongated denial of maternal alcoholism may account for the average age at which adult children of two alcoholic parents acknowledged the condition. It would seem that having two alcoholic parents would be acknowledged more quickly than having one. However, the delay in accepting maternal alcoholism appears to increase the average age in the case of two alcoholic parents. Another factor to consider in the case of two alcoholic parents is that the alcoholism may not have developed at the same time in both parents.

The last issues about age and its diversity of effects on adult children of alcoholics are concerned with how old you are now. These age considerations raise two issues. One is what are the normal developmental issues that all people your age normally experience? Two, are the problems for adult children of alcoholism more likely to become apparent at particular ages, and if so, at what age?

Initially, the adult child must be able to separate what are normal developmental issues of adulthood, such as intimacy, generativity (which is the ability to give beyond yourself to the next generation), a sense of integrity and the ability to self-actualize. These issues are difficult in themselves for all adults, let alone for adult children of alcoholics who will experience these as well as a variety of other issues related to parental alcoholism.

Thus adult children will bring their own set of unique age issues related to parental alcoholism not unlike those of young children and adolescents of alcoholics. It is important to recognize at this point, however, that the adult child will have a combination of issues to confront. These will be a combination of normal developmental concerns and the unique concerns of being an adult child of an alcoholic plus how these two areas combine to impede, arrest or accelerate the human developmental process. Additionally, some of these will be carried over from childhood or adolescence, and others will develop in adulthood.

At what age in adulthood are they most likely to manifest themselves? Table 2.9 compares the scores of adult children of alcoholics with adults of non-alcoholic parents at different ages for the degree to which they possess the personality characteristics which have been identified with adult children of alcoholics used in previous tables (see previous tables for the personality characteristics). Not only does this table indicate at

Table 2.10

Differences in Personality Characteristics by Age in Adult Children of Alcoholics and Adults of Non-Alcoholic Parents

Age Group

	Under 25	26-35	36-45	46-55	56+

Personality Characteristic Scores

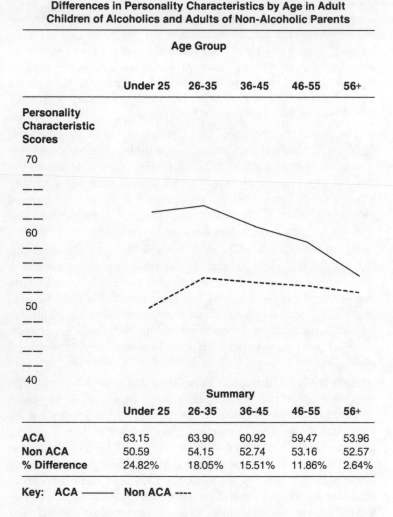

Summary

	Under 25	26-35	36-45	46-55	56+
ACA	63.15	63.90	60.92	59.47	53.96
Non ACA	50.59	54.15	52.74	53.16	52.57
% Difference	24.82%	18.05%	15.51%	11.86%	2.64%

Key: ACA ——— Non ACA ----

what ages the characteristics are most noticeable, but also at what ages the differences between adult children and adults in general are the greatest (see Table 2.10).

As indicated in Table 2.10 adult children of alcoholics are most affected until their mid-thirties, at which time the degree to which they were affected begins to decline. Additionally, it is during these years that the greatest differences between adult children and adults of non-alcoholic parents are apparent. These years, however, for most adults are highly transitional years regarding careers, families and relationships, but for adult children of alcoholics the normal stresses of these years may accentuate the many personality characteristics from difficult childhoods.

Thus the stresses of childhood may be particularly noticeable during the stresses of adulthood. It is interesting to note that as both groups mature and some of the transitional stresses are eliminated, the differences will begin to disappear until finally the two groups almost merge.

The age factor is highly related to the concept of "recovery lag", in which not all parts of the individual will need the same degree of intervention nor will all parts of the individual recover at the same rate. It is possible that the adult child will need to work on different issues that occurred at different ages in his or her life particularly if these issues have remained largely unresolved. Thus the adult child finds himself or herself emotionally impacted by experiences that occurred at different ages of their lives.

A positive side of this for adult children, however, is that at this point in their lives they may now possess more emotional support and interpersonal skills for resolving issues than they possessed when they were younger. Thus the motto of "survive now and heal later" may make more sense, since now the adult may have more resources for understanding and resolving issues that he or she was not previously capable of handling.

As a young child of an alcoholic, your age may have worked against you and kept you from being able to seek help or resolve issues, but as an adult you can now use your age as an asset to release any negative childhood experiences. Again, this task will be a process with many factors influencing the outcome, but certainly age is one of the main factors. The longer your exposure to active alcoholism, the higher the probability that it will have produced more issues for you to resolve.

An adult child whose parent became alcoholic when the child was ten and then achieved sobriety when the child was twenty-two, may have very different feelings than an adult child who was born into an alcoholic home and whose parent is still drinking. Additionally, for the few fortunate adult children whose parent has quit drinking, age still may be a factor. For example, how old were you when the parent became sober?

In the national study, the average age of adult children whose parent became sober was 24.3 years. These adult children may have entirely different perceptions, issues and attitudes about parental alcoholism than adult children whose parents have never stopped drinking, thus the adult child has never had the opportunity to know the alcoholic parent sober.

7. Offsetting Factors

Not all variations of effects on adult children of alcoholics can be easily understood. Many differences in effects may be due to unknown or "offsetting factors" in the adult child's life. These offsetting factors may be other people or institutions that have had a positive effect on the adult child either now or when the adult was growing up. What these individuals or institutions accomplished either knowingly or unknowingly was that they were able to provide the adult child with positive role models, emotional support, meaningful activities, a sense of belonging or simply a much needed diversion from the family conflict.

It is difficult to assess the impact of offsetting factors, but for the adult child it is important to realize the positive impact that they may have had on the adult child's life. The importance of the offsetting person or institution for the adult child may be that it was able to help provide a "balance" in the adult child's life.

For example, school may have been an offsetting factor for some adult children because it provided not only a break physically from family involvement, but also an emotional recess from thinking about the family. Additionally, for those adult children who did well in school or felt that they belonged socially, the school experience may have been able to provide a positive self-concept that was not offered in the home.

Another aspect of offsetting factors involves the importance of primary relationships in one's life. For adult children of alcoholics who remember having close and primary relationships outside of the family, the impact of the alcoholism may have been reduced, since they had an identity that was separate from the alcoholism. However, for adult children who were withdrawn and physically or emotionally isolated, the impact of the parental alcoholism may have been felt even more severely. An adult child who had friends and belonged to several organizations or groups, had the opportunity to have meaningful interactions during his or her day. The "loner" child, however, only increased the degree of isolation already felt by most children of alcoholics because of a lack of outside support systems.

Besides belonging to institutions or groups, adult children may have had a particular person who was a significant individual in his or her life who helped reduce the impact of parental alcoholism. This may have been a sibling, other relative, best friend or an adult who interacted positively with the adult child. It is possible that this could have been the non-alcoholic parent as well.

In a study in Poland on adult children of alcoholics, it was found that among those adult children who were now doing well in their lives, as opposed to those who were not, the intervening variable that made a difference was that the adult children who were doing well all had a very positive image of how their non-alcoholic parent fulfilled his or her role as parent (Obuchowska, 1974). Thus the non-alcoholic parent's ability to fulfill the parental role successfully served as a significant offsetting factor for the alcoholic parent's impact. In Table 2.11 the percentage of adult children who stated they were able to share their feelings with someone about the parental alcoholism is indicated.

Table 2.11

Percent of Adult Children of Alcoholics Who Received Help With Their Feelings

Received help	10.8%
Did not receive help	89.2%

Unfortunately, as indicated on Table 2.11, the vast majority of adult children did not receive help from anyone while they were growing up with their feelings. This does not mean, however, that offsetting factors did not occur. As stated earlier, they could have been directly or indirectly received.

For the adult child, what kinds of activities or persons can they identify as "contributing others" in their lives? What benefits did they derive from interaction with others who helped them maintain an emotional balance? This may have been accomplished in the adult child's life, even though those with whom he or she interacted did not know the "family secret". On the other hand, there were those with whom you could share the family secret and from whom you could derive support, even though the situation was not resolved. It is important, therefore, for the adult child to realize that the offsetting factors were indeed positive and that establishing them and maintaining them now may continue to serve the adult child with a positive sense of identity, support and acceptance.

8. Cultural Considerations

All of us possess individual and family differences, some of which are genetically inherited and others which are socially inherited. These differences include our race, ethnicity, religions, values and family norms. It is important to take these variables into consideration for adult children of alcoholics because the adult child (like all children) was raised in his or her own particular social context. Thus, a Black adult child may have similar experiences to Hispanic or White adult children but at the same time may have different experiences related to alcoholism in the Black community which the others did not experience. The same is true for other groups.

Again the experience of parental alcoholism may be common, but how each family's system of values, race, ethnic composition and religion respond may indicate the need for appreciation for cultural considerations. For example, is it different to be a child of an alcoholic in a family where the religion forbids the use of any alcohol, as opposed to being in an alcoholic family that does not? Does alcoholism affect the minority family more, less or differently than it does majority families?

In most societies, the further you are away from the average or the norm in the society, the more other societal issues will impact on you and your family. If you represent the average in your society, however, most of the societal norms and practices represent your orientation. Thus the majority adult child may not have the "extra issues" to accompany his or her status that a minority adult child may bring into focus. The minority adult child may have many of the same feelings and can identify with the issues affecting all adult children, but he or she may also have the additional considerations of being a minority.

Alcoholism does not affect all groups the same. There are differences in rates of prevalence, gender, recovery and utilization of human services for intervention. Table 2.12 indicates the differences in scores of adult children by race in the United States (see Table 2.12).

Additionally, Table 2.12 indicates the differences among each race between adults with alcoholic parents and those with non-alcoholic parents. These differences are apparent in the scores

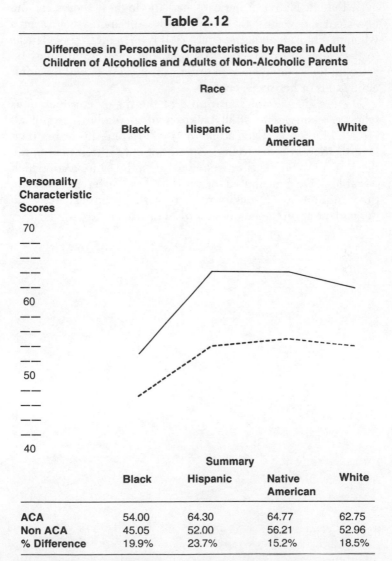

Table 2.12

Differences in Personality Characteristics by Race in Adult Children of Alcoholics and Adults of Non-Alcoholic Parents

	Black	Hispanic	Native American	White
Summary				
ACA	54.00	64.30	64.77	62.75
Non ACA	45.05	52.00	56.21	52.96
% Difference	19.9%	23.7%	15.2%	18.5%

Key: ACA _____ Non ACA ....

of adults with non-alcoholics parents, in which Blacks possessed the personality characteristics the least and Native Americans identified with them the most. When parental alcoholism was considered this pattern remained the same. Hispanics with alcoholic parents had the greatest increase in personality characteristics, followed in order by Blacks, Whites and Native Americans over adults with non-alcoholic parents. Additionally, even though Native Americans had the highest scores for the non-alcoholic group, they had the lowest increase in scores when parental alcoholism occurred. It is difficult to speculate as to the cause in differences in scores, but each group must be assessed for its uniqueness in order to fully understand the adult child in his or her social context.

These eight variables are some of the major considerations when assessing why adult children of alcoholics are not all affected the same. Each adult child will require his or her own investigation in order to understand not only differences in the degrees to which he or she was affected, but also which variables have contributed the most to these differences. Again, the uniqueness of the journey towards recovery may be dependent upon the uniqueness of the path already traveled.

3

Making Peace
With Reality

What does it mean to be an adult child of an alcoholic? What
is implied overtly and covertly by the phrase "adult children of
alcoholics"? Each adult child will need to come to terms not
only with these questions, but also with his or her current status
as an adult child. Much of this depends upon the adult child
being able to accept and make peace with the reality that he or
she is, in fact, a child of an alcoholic. This will require looking
at one's past, understanding the implications for saying that one
is an adult child, working through the common feelings that will
arise, and being willing to develop an identity beyond your past.

Co-dependence or Co-existence?

There are two aspects about one's past that remain constant.
One, your past did happen to you. Two, the best thing about a
negative past is that it is past. However, even though some of it
may be over physically, such as the period of childhood, the
emotional impact may not be over. Thus the adult child is faced
with being either co-dependent upon the past, allowing many of

the negative implications to persist, or learning to co-exist with the past.

Co-dependence often is used to describe the behaviors and attitudes of those living with an alcoholic. The co-dependent person is one who gives up his or her own sense of healthy independence and power to another. It is a one-directional relationship in which the co-dependent person is always a reactor to someone else's acting. Thus, the alcoholic was the actor, and the non-alcoholic family members became the reactors. Another way of looking at co-dependency, however, would be to state that the adult child is co-dependent upon his or her past and that he or she has a one-directional relationship again. This happens when current behavior is not present or future-motivated, but instead is past-directed. The adult child who overly identifies with the past is overly dependent upon it and thus is co-dependent.

The negative aspects of the past need to be released, but it is naive to assume that just by saying "I will not be influenced by my past" that the past will disappear and all of its influences with it. The adult child is faced with a choice of either abandoning the co-dependency on the past or allowing it to become the eternal yesterday by letting go to achieve a co-existence with one's past. Co-existence means admitting that it happened to you, that it exists and that you exist.

The crucial question is can you co-exist? The key to co-existence is dependent upon a minimum of two issues. One is acceptance of the past. It is important, however, to remember that acceptance does not mean approval. It merely means that you are willing to acknowledge reality. It is difficult to deal fully with a situation that you acknowledge only partially. It is like saying I want to recover fully, but I wasn't actually injured. The adult child is stating, I am 100% aware of my *desire* to recover, but only 50% aware of my *need* to recover.

The second issue involves the adult child who still wants the past to be different. Stop wanting your life in the past to be different, and start making it different now. Wanting your past to be different and spending all of your emotional energy on it will rob you of the energy needed to improve the present. However, much of your ability to improve the present will depend upon your ability to achieve a position of neutrality with your past.

Again, keep in mind that acceptance does not mean approval, but it will allow you to acknowledge exactly what you are attempting to recover from and to understand your feelings. In doing this, many feelings and implications for acknowledging your status as an adult child will arise. Not all adult children will feel the same about or have the same implications from their past. Each must explore the individual meaning for himself or herself which comes with acknowledging he or she is an adult child.

What Does It Mean to be an Adult Child?

There are a variety of issues, feelings and implications that may arise for someone who admits, "I am an adult child of an alcoholic". It is important to understand that acknowledging your past stimulates many feelings from the past and about the present. These feelings must be appreciated to understand the adult child's position. The following are implications that may arise for an adult child who states that not only am I an adult child of an alcoholic, but also I am feeling these implications about my present status.

1. If you admit you are an adult child, does that imply you have overcome denial?

If acknowledging that one is an alcoholic is so critical to overcoming denial of alcoholism, why is it any less significant for the child of the alcoholic to acknowledge? Denial of parental alcoholism needs to be worked through carefully, as does understanding that implications in overcoming denial are important. Additional factors may include how long the adult child has denied the status, or what has been the motivation for the denial. Why someone denies may be even more critical than the denial itself.

As mentioned in chapter one, I have met more adult children of alcoholics whose brothers and sisters are not adult children. This denial of parental alcoholism and overcoming it thus raises not only the issues inherent in the denial issue itself, but also is related to all of the other implications. Overcoming denial and accepting reality may take time. After all, having been exposed to active alcoholism for years, overcoming denial in a short period may not allow sufficient time for the adult child to process all of the implications and motivations associated with long-term denial. Understanding that one is denying and overcoming denial may be two entirely different issues that require not only separating them, but also realizing that it is normal to allow time between becoming aware and acting on that awareness.

2. If you admit you are an adult child, does that imply you have come to terms with the word "alcoholic"?

What images and connotations do you associate with the word alcoholic? For many people, alcoholism unfortunately carries the connotation of immoral or socially unacceptable behavior. Does accepting you are the adult child of an alcoholic mean you understand alcoholism as a disease?

A woman in an adult children's group asked a very insightful question. She stated to the group in all sincerity that "alcoholism is a disease, right?" and the group agreed. Then she said, "And my dad was alcoholic, therefore he has alcoholism." Again, the group agreed. Her question to the group then was, "What do I have?" At this point the group went into discussion of many issues with little consensus, but with some concept of the term "alcoholic".

The adult child also may feel that the very existence of negative associations with alcoholism also reflects negatively on the child simply because they are part of "that family", as opposed to having an identity as an individual. Coming to terms with the word alcoholic may mean that the adult child has come to accept that alcoholism existed or exists, as opposed to having convinced himself or herself that it was "problem drinking", rather than alcoholism. One rationalization with which some adult children may identify is the feeling that the parent was not alcoholic because he or she was "not that bad yet". This meant that there must have been some image of what constituted an alcoholic and, if this image was sufficiently negative, that it further increased the motivation for denial. Thus children of alcoholics, like others in general, have their own interpretations of the word alcoholic and all that it does or does not imply.

3. If you admit you are an adult child, does that imply that your parent is or was an alcoholic?

As mentioned in chapter two, it is one thing to say that the neighbor is an alcoholic and it is entirely different to say that one or both of your parents is alcoholic. Children are hesitant to make negative statements about their parents. Not only may it be difficult to admit to yourself that you have an alcoholic parent, but admitting it to others may be even more painful.

4. If you admit you are an adult child, does that imply that you are saying good-bye to the parents you never had?

It is difficult to accept that the people with whom you live or love may have had a negative impact on you. Additionally, you may tend to deny the extent of harm that another individual may have inflicted on you, and the degree of your denial may be related to how close you were or are to the person. That is, the closer you are to an individual, the more you may deny the degree of the harm he or she has inflicted.

This is a very common syndrome in abusive families, in which abused spouses or children actually will deny or rationalize the extent of harm by the perpetrator if they are particularly close to this individual. There is a theoretical argument that looks at this issue from the victim's point of view and theorizes that the closer the victim is emotionally to the perpetrator, the greater the degree of emotional harm done to the victim. Thus, adult children who accept the reality of their past may need to say good-bye simultaneously to the images of their parents that do not correspond with reality. All children may possess two sets of parents. One is the internalized parent, that is, the child's "ideal" of how parents should be and which the child looks for in his or her parent. The other parent for the child is the "real" parent, the one evident in the actual behavior of the parent.

Some adult children will have a closer correspondence between their ideal and real parent, whereas others will experience a great disparity between the two images. This disparity however, usually stems from two forms of misperception. In one case, there is the adult child who does not have a correct perception of the parent because it is too idealized. In the other case, the adult child carries a too literal perception of the real parent which is extremely negative and overly sensitive to every action of the parent.

The image and need for an ideal parental relationship may be so strong for some adult children, however, that accepting the fact that one's parent is actually an alcoholic may mean that the adult child must give up the parent that he or she has created, which may mean giving up one of the key components of survival to date. It also is part of the syndrome of wanting the past to be different. When the adult child realizes and accepts the reality of the parent, however, he or she does not have to approve of it.

For many adult children, accepting reality by saying good-bye to the parent(s) that they never had, will help them achieve an emotionally neutral position about the parental impacts of alcoholism. Some adult children will not be able or willing to go beyond this point because of their inability to genuinely forgive. Other adult children not only will be able to say good-bye to the parents they never had, but also will attempt to understand better the ones they do have.

5. If you admit you are an adult child, does that imply you are willing to say "hello" to the parents you do have?

This implication addresses the level of acceptance for adult children of their parents, once parental alcoholism is admitted. It parallels the issue of saying good-bye and at the same time it goes beyond it. Saying good-bye to an idealized parent involves coming to terms with real parent(s). The implication in saying hello is not only accepting the parent you do have, but also facing the question of your willingness to interact with your real parent(s) and even to grow beyond neutrality in your relationship with them.

Again, as some adult children never will be able to forgive, others will. Still others will be able to go beyond forgiveness. Accepting and interacting with your parents beyond forgiveness will be discussed in more detail in Chapter Five.

However, it is important to remember that acknowledging one's status as an adult child will have the implications that the parental relationships never were or may never be what the adult child would prefer. We have only one childhood and we usually have only one set of parental relationships. Many adult children would like to have only one congruent image of both, but may have created an ideal that helps to protect them from the real image that may cause emotional pain. Bringing the two images together into an accurate perception and then achieving acceptance of this perception will be a great emotional challenge for many adult children.

6. *If you admit you are an adult child, does that imply you are accepting reality, even though you may live with a fantasy about your life?*

The preceding two implications were directly concerned with the images of your parents, but what about your images of yourself and your own life? Does acceptance of an adult child status change your reality? If you have maintained high degrees of denial in areas of your life affected by parental alcoholism, acknowledgement may mean facing accepting yourself and how you are actually living today. This issue may have its origins in childhood because it may have been easier to handle parental alcoholism by replacing reality with fantasy. If reality is accepted, the fantasy not only is abandoned, but also it is no longer available to help avoid adult realities.

7. *If you admit you are an adult child, does that imply you no longer are normal?*

It is ironic that the adult child may not want to acknowledge his or her status because it may carry the implication that he or she no longer is normal, yet the adult child may have spent much of his or her life trying to convince himself or herself and others that he or she is normal. This lifelong effort to deny reality can be interpreted as an emotional trap. By not acknowledging you are an adult child, you can remain "normal" even though you feel different. But doesn't acknowledging being an adult child mean that you are "different" but pretending you are normal? You may well wonder if the mixed messages of alcoholism ever stop. Perhaps they do or at least are diminished, but to achieve this it becomes necessary to stop maintaining two separate forms of reality for yourself. Besides, what does it mean to be normal anyway? Do you realize that reacting abnormally in an abnormal situation may be normal?

A basic premise of this book is that not all parts of an adult child nor all adult children are affected to the same degree or in the same areas. Therefore, take comfort in the knowledge that some parts of you are normal. OK, I forgot, "perfectly" normal.

A good example of the mixed messages experienced by many adult children concern their perception of what constitutes normal behavior. What they perceive as normal for others is not normal for them, thus they perceive two different levels of reality. Maintaining one consistent reality is difficult enough for most people, so put away your incredible levels of competency and allow yourself the luxury of only one "normal" reality. Working within one level of competence and one reality is more realistic and contains more potential for your own growth. By maintaining two, you will impede your growth in both, and neither of the realities will be the normal you. Start your identity consolidation by acknowledging your status and recognizing that feeling different not only is permissible but also is normal. It is *okay* to be an adult child of an alcoholic. There are over 28 million adult children of alcoholics in this country, surely the largest "group" of unique individuals I have ever met.

8. *If you admit you are an adult child, does that imply you have been affected?*

It is difficult to survive a chaotic childhood and then be confronted with the implication that in spite of your efforts at survival, you may have negative residual effects. Thus parental alcoholism should not be viewed by the adult child as a reflection on the alcoholic parent only, but also as a revelation about the adult child. It is one thing to assess the impact of exposure to alcoholism, it is another to assess the effects on yourself, particularly if you feel you now possess negative characteristics.

9. *If you admit you are an adult child, does that imply that you cannot be on your own successfully and no longer be affected?*

This implication is for those adult children who feel that in spite of their past, they have been able to overcome any negative impacts and have achieved successful lives. Does acknowledging your status mean you are not as healthy as you think? This is not necessarily so, but it is easy to see why many adult children may think this way.

Much emphasis today on adult children's issues consistently focuses only on the negative characteristics adult children may have developed. The fact that the adult children are survivors and often possess strong and viable social skills often is overlooked. Additionally, there are many adult children, as there are adults from other types of dysfunctional families, who have overcome negative childhoods to achieve positive adulthoods. Some adult children may feel they have struggled to get where they are but by officially acknowledging their status, they will be pulled back into what they have overcome. Others may feel that they have resolved some issues, but fear that acknowledgment may raise questions about how well these issues have been resolved, thus fearing an emotional relapse. If the adult child actually has overcome these issues and feels emotionally and socially successful, then he or she will not be intimidated by acknowledgment.

10. If you admit you are an adult child, does that imply you must bring up your past?

This implication is related not only to bringing up the past but the attitude of "Why bring up the past? It's over, and besides there are too many painful memories." Thus the motivation for not wanting to acknowledge one's status may stem from not wanting to be confronted with past memories. One comfort for the adult child may be that if you survived living the experience, you have the strength to survive remembering it. Another observation is that the past is over and there is nothing to be gained from remembering it. What the adult child must honestly ask is, "Is the past over for me in a satisfactory way?" If it is, then bringing up the past no longer will be necessary, nor will the fear of too many painful memories or the fear of the past create anxiety.

11. If you admit you are an adult child of a recovering alcoholic parent, does that imply it no longer is justifiable to talk about it?

Unfortunately, not enough adult children have the "luxury" of emotionally confronting this problem because too few alcoholics are in recovery. For those adult children whose parent is recovering, however, how justifiable is it to state that you are a child of an alcoholic? In my opinion, it is totally appropriate and just as meaningful as it is for the recovering alcoholic to state that he or she is an alcoholic. The stopping of active drinking does not cause the issues, feelings and implications of the experience to disappear.

Additionally, adult children of recovering alcoholics could find themselves in a no-win situation if they feel that during the active drinking they could not talk about it, and now during sobriety they still cannot talk about it. It is the "silence before and the silence after" syndrome, with no appreciation for what has occurred during the silence. Many recovering alcoholic parents become concerned about what effects they may have had on their children, yet when they bring up the subject of their active drinking behavior, it is the children who are uncomfortable in talking about it. There is a wonderful statement in the Desiderata which applies to adult children of alcoholics; it says, "You have a right to be here."

12. If you admit you are an adult child, does that imply since it has been acknowledged, you must deal with your feelings?

This implication is an interesting trap for some adult children. "If you acknowledge it, do you have to deal with it?" becomes a question that raises many issues. The response for some adult children is not to acknowledge it so they do not have to deal with it. Thus it is not the acknowledgment the adult child confronts, but rather the fear of having to handle the feelings which may come with it.

One way to handle it is not to. An interesting question this choice raises for the adult child is, "Do you handle it, or does it handle you?" Each adult child will need to assess his or her response to this possible consequence of the need to confront or not to confront his or her feelings.

13. If you admit you are an adult child, does that imply you have betrayed someone?

Central to acknowledging one's status as an adult child is dealing with one's anxiety about betrayal. This could involve betraying the "family secret", the alcoholic, your siblings, yourself or the non-alcoholic parent who tried to protect you. Many family members in an alcoholic home become enmeshed in maintaining boundaries about information regarding their family. Although this enmeshment may maintain negative behaviors, violating the no-talk rule will make the person a traitor and thus an outsider in the family. In this situation one way to belong is to "go along". That is, no one talks about what is happening in the family in order to stay part of the system. Claudia Black often refers to these unwritten rules as the "don't talk, don't trust and don't feel" guidelines that emerge in many addictive families (Black, 1982). Saying that you are an adult child not only may challenge these rules, but also may brand the adult child as an outsider.

Another issue of betrayal may involve the adult child and the non-alcoholic parent. This may be especially true in situations where the non-alcoholic parent feels he or she "protected" the adult child. If the adult child admits his or her status, does this mean to the non-alcoholic parent that he or she was not able to protect the child? This puts the adult child in an awkward position, and not wanting to hurt the non-alcoholic parent becomes the motivation for denial. Many times adult children who are in support groups for parental alcoholism hope their family members do not find out that they are in a group.

14. If you admit you are an adult child, does that imply your relationship with the non-alcoholic parent or any siblings will be affected?

This is a very powerful concern for adult children, especially in families where there is still individual denial about alcoholism. Often this situation will lead to a debate over whether the parent really is or was alcoholic, which then creates distance between the family members. Adult children's growth does not depend upon the validation of others before it can occur. It would be nice to have the support and validation from your siblings that your feelings and insights are justifiable, but it is not a prerequisite to your growth. Just as you may have to work through what all of these implications mean to you so, too, will your siblings.

Another issue is that adult children are not responsible for the recovery of their siblings or non-alcoholic parent. This is another aspect of the trap of assuming too much responsibility, particularly over a situation over which you have no control anyway. You cannot recover for another person. Remember your acknowledgment may be threatening to others because they may feel it is a reflection upon them or it implies they too should seek recovery.

15. If you admit you are an adult child, does that imply others will know this about you?

Each adult child will need to assess the implication of revelation about his or her status. This may depend upon your relationship to the person to whom you are making the disclosure. For example, there are great differences in what best friends or relatives know about us, as opposed to employers, employees or casual friendships. In most cases, you control information about your family life. In the case of best friends, telling them you are an adult child is probably not news to them. They observed it all along; you just never talked about it.

Another disclosure criterion may be yourself. The further along you are with your own recovery, the less intimidating your acknowledgment may be. Since there are so many adult children, your disclosure may generate the increasingly common response, "I'm an adult child, too." You are not alone unless you choose to be. Depending upon your own level of growth, choose your revelations wisely.

16. If you admit you are an adult child, does that imply you must confront the alcoholic?

This is one of the most powerful implications for many adult children. Do I have to confront the alcoholic? Do I have to get him or her into treatment? The answer is No! Children of alcoholics cannot get sober for their parent. Yes, you say, but I should do this or I should do that. Look at it this way. If you could get sober for your parent, you probably would have done it long ago. You do not "have to" confront the alcoholic. However, you may feel that you "need" to confront the alcoholic. That is different because your need stems from choice, not from an unrealistic sense of responsibilty. Your own recovery must come first. To do otherwise is to accept that as long as their alcoholism endures, you can do nothing for yourself except to continue to endure their alcoholism. Your recovery is not dependent upon their parents' sobriety, just as the parents' sobriety is not dependent upon your recovery.

You may choose to confront or not confront the alcoholic. This is a separate issue from confronting your own status, but if you do choose confrontation, you choose the time, depending upon your level of growth, acceptance and forgiveness. Other adult children may not choose to confront the alcoholic because they are too bitter or feel hypocritical about offering forgiveness or acceptance when they neither forgive nor accept. Finally, there are those adult children whose alcoholic parent is no longer available to them or has died. Confronting the alcoholic is not a prerequsite to confronting yourself.

Throughout the process of confronting yourself, many feelings will arise which you will need to resolve, feelings similar to the ones shared by adults who were victimized as children by abuse, neglect or incest (Gil, 1984). The adult child looking back at his or her childhood may feel very much victimized and must be able to work through the feelings of victimization. The mind of an adult child is an emotional storage bin of all of the past experiences, behaviors, implications and feelings of childhood. However, releasing and understanding these feelings and implications may be related to how openly the adult child is willing to acknowledge the feelings. Just as implications for one's status may not have been considered, the accompanying feelings may not be considered because of the fact that the adult child may knowingly or unknowingly be blocking the acknowledgement of his or her memories. This usually occurs because of denial, definitional problems, minimizing, rationalization or selective memory, all of which contribute to the adult child's ability or lack of ability to accept reality.

Acceptance of reality, therefore, depends upon the degree to which you will allow your memory to be accurate. Adult children can sabotage or weaken the acceptance process by convincing themselves that they have accepted all of their experiences when, in fact, they have not. Not only have they again altered what was real, but also they have chosen to redefine the situation while they are accepting it. Thus we find adult children who say they have dealt with or accepted their past, but are still plagued by the "eternal yesterday" because *all* of yesterday was not allowed to be acknowledged. The cognitive processes of denial, definitional problems, minimizing, rationalizing, and selective memory contribute to this problem.

Denial

Critical to accepting reality is the degree of denial involved about that reality. It may not be as important for the adult child to have exact recall of reality as it is to be willing to remember. All of the cognitive processes involve some form of denial. Whether it is denying that a parent was alcoholic, that you were affected or that your family was not as close as you pretend, your denial mechanism may be operating to protect you from reality.

Denial does not necessarily mean that you would not seek intervention under the facade of some other issue. For example, an adult repeatedly may experience relationship problems and seek help, yet refuse to consider the fact that being an adult child has anything to do with the situation. This may explain why only 5% of adult children are in any intervention just for being adult children of alcoholics, and yet the majority of case loads of many clinicians are adult children of alcoholics.

Adult children *are* showing up in intervention programs, but for problems other than being adult children. This could be caused by denial of parental alcoholism and its effects on other problems, denial of any adult children's problems, denial that one's childhood may affect one's adulthood or a combination of these.

The Definition Debate

The definition debate involves whether or not you define a situation as real. Does the situation fit your definition of what you are talking about? Alcoholism is one of the classic examples for the debate process. The adult child may be more willing to say that the parent was a "problem drinker" than an "alcoholic", because the two are defined differently by the adult child. Part of making peace with reality is also making peace with the definition of that reality. The closer one is to the person being defined, the more difficult to accept that definition. Many adult children may find themselves mentally arguing whether the parent "really" was alcoholic or was it something else? Paramount to this debate are the tendencies to minimize a behavior and rationalize its existence.

Minimizing

Minimizing is the process of reducing the impact that the alcoholic's behavior may have had on you. Such statements as "It really wasn't that bad" or "He did what he wanted, but it didn't affect me", may be used in an attempt to underestimate the consequences of parental alcoholism. For the adult child who feels he or she finally has things under control, but has never accepted the alcoholism, minimizing not only the existence of alcoholism, but also any negative effects, keeps the adult child from testing the strength of his or her recovery.

A good example of minimizing is when you actually state that, "It really didn't bother me" or "It doesn't bother me now", when in fact you feel like admitting that "Yes, that did hurt" or "Yes, it still bothers me".

Minimizing one's past can be a very internal process in which you convince yourself mentally and emotionally that you were not affected. People normally do not minimize insignificant behaviors because that would be unnecessary. For many adult children admitting the need to minimize the exposure to parental alcoholism may help them realize and acknowledge they are attempting to reduce the impact of a significant behavior on their lives.

Rationalization

Rationalization is the process of explaining a behavior to make it either reasonable or justifiable. Additionally, it involves making the irrational appear rational. Critical to the process is the fact it involves not only rationalizing your own behavior, but also the behaviors of others. Thus justification of a behavior can involve not only the person who performs the act, but also another individual who may justify it for the performer.

For example, the adult child may attempt to rationalize a parent's excessive drinking by thinking or saying that it really is not the drinking that is problematic, but rather what is causing the drinking. Thus the adult child rationalizes that the parent does not have a drinking problem but is having problems somewhere else, and the drinking is either a solution to the problem or an unfortunate by-product.

Another form involves the adult child rationalizing that what has happened is somehow justified. The rationalizing adult child attempts to find any plausible explanation to explain his or her childhood, even though the reasons may not be true. Rationalization may help one understand why a parent is alcoholic, but keep the adult child from having a clear picture of reality. Too much rationalization will add to the mixed messages and confusion usually accompanying alcoholic parents.

If the adult child rationalizes a behavior to the point of justification, does this mean that the adult child cannot have negative effects from the behavior? Does this justification make the need or desire for recovery unjustified? Why would you recover from something that reasonably occurred? Thus the adult child who overly justifies finds himself or herself, not only confusing reality, but also of undermining the legitimacy of the need for intervention.

Selective Memory

Selective memory involves two processes for the adult child. One is remembering only what you want to and the other is remembering a behavior differently from how it actually happened. Again, both of these processes challenge reality and the acceptance of it. The adult child may contend that not only has he or she made peace with reality, but also that it was not that difficult. This same adult child, however, keeps experiencing a fragile mental peace. Is it possible that what really happened is the adult child made peace only with the selective memory and other issues have been ignored? This does not condemn totally having a selective memory. Much of the experience of making peace with reality is a process that will occur in stages. It is possible one will not remember everything at one time or choose not to work on all one's memories at the same time. As you grow, you allow yourself to face issues that up to then you continued to have denied. Another indicator of growth may be that memories that once were very painful now can be recalled with less and less pain. They do not come back as strong any more, because not only have you worked through some of the emotional pain, but also you are now a stronger person than when you first overcame your selective memory.

Letting Go of Your Past

How do you escape your past? You don't. It is part of you,
but you can choose which part of you. Either you can allow your
past to dominate totally both present and future, or you can
subjugate it to become a minor part of your identity. You had no
choice and little control over your childhood, but you have both
over your adulthood. The choice begins with letting go of your
past. Either your past can control you emotionally or you can
learn to control it emotionally. Learning to control the emotional
impact of the past will depend upon the degree of impact, your
own efforts, availability of support systems and time. It is not an
easy process and will require accepting and remembering
where you have been and assessing where you want to go. As
you achieve greater personal understanding, insight and growth,
you should say to yourself, "I am an adult child, but more
importantly I am becoming . . ."

The following are some suggestions for the adult child who
wishes to make peace with the past.

1. Assess where you are now.

You may want to use the personality assessment scales in
Chapter One to help you get a better understanding of yourself.
Have you accepted the feelings which kept you from acknowledging your status or have now arisen since you overcame
denial? If you are still reading this book, you may have
intellectually and cognitively accepted your status, but what
about emotionally?

2. Truly understand that acceptance does not mean approval.

Much of making peace with reality means that you have
emotionally achieved a position of neutrality. This does not
imply that you do not have other positive or negative feelings,
but that you accept that they are real. Besides accepting that one
had or has an alcoholic parent is more logical. Unfortunately,
our approval is not a prerequisite for the existence of this
condition.

3. Stop wanting it to be different.

This desire must be abandoned and replaced with accepting
the past. Holding onto this wish keeps you from being oriented
toward the present and suggests that since the past cannot be
different, then you cannot change. The reality is you *can* change
yourself. You cannot change the past.

4. Stop doing what you do not do.

At first this statement seems contradictory but it is not. What it means is to quit the habits that keep you locked into limited alternatives.

For example, you do not believe things can change, you do not share the family secret, you do not believe you have been affected, you do not take an active interest in yourself, you do not seek support or you do not acknowledge your status. All of these things will maintain your negative patterns of emotional and physical inactivity, and thus you will increase you attachment to your past by your passive acceptance and behavior. By doing nothing you may be unknowingly maintaining what you really want to abandon. One thing you can be sure of, if you do absolutely nothing, then nothing will happen to improve your life. Stop doing nothing.

5. Let go of the "if onlys".

Statements such as, "If only I had done this", or "If only I had done that, this would not have happened", keep you tied to the past. "If only" implies that you could have made it different or that somehow you were responsible for the parent's drinking. It keeps you second guessing yourself and holds you unrealistically accountable for something over which you had no control. Replace "if only" statements with "I will" statements. "I will" asserts that you have an active role in determining who you are and frees you from accusing yourself of what you "should have done", even though you could not have stopped parental alcoholism anyway.

6. Do not overcompensate for your past.

You may as well fall flat on your face as bend too far backwards. Either way you wind up in a position you do not want. For adult children overcompensating for the past may be related to alcoholizing all behavior. Constantly being on guard to control your past means your past is still in control. As you begin to let go and accept reality, you no longer will need to compensate, because you will begin to see yourself in the context of what is, as opposed to what has been. Recovering adult children are attempting to reach emotional balance in their lives. As children they may have adapted to the parental alcoholism, which resulted in childhood equilibrium being upset. Overcompensating in adulthood for a childhood imbalance results in adulthood being imbalanced. As past influences are reduced, present influences can become stronger.

7. Be here, be now.

Past resentments can rob us not only of the present, but also of the future. These resentments consume much needed energy to handle today, and the person who clings to resentments begins each day without a full range of resources. Using your energy today to handle the past may make handling today that much more difficult. The adult child who is able to make peace with reality is freeing enormous amounts of energy to improve his or her life. By being here and being now, the adult person can use all of his or her emotional resources in the present. If you are going to improve your life now, you need to have all of your emotional resources currently available. Thus the adult child in recovery who has been able to make peace with his or her past is the one who can say honestly "I am an adult child of an alcoholic, and I am becoming . . ."

4

Making Peace With Yourself

It is difficult to be in conflict internally and to be at peace externally. Not being at peace with yourself will impair your ability to be at peace with others. Some adult children may be engaging in such behaviors as constantly placating others, giving but not receiving, always being the one to maintain a relationship or putting their needs second to others, even though they resent these behaviors. They are locked into behaviors that they feel will maintain an external peace, yet unknowingly maintain their own dissonance.

The adult child who wants to recover must be able to make peace with himself/herself. Not being able to do this will undermine all of the other attempts at growth. The adult child may feel he or she has dealt with many of the issues or individuals from the past; but, if the adult child has not achieved true inner peace, any external attempts will be the same as the above behavior, where the adult child is doing everything for everyone else and nothing for himself or herself. The adult child will be maintaining the same behavior which existed in the alcoholic family and which led to the adult child putting his or her feelings second in order to maintain a sense of situational balance. The result is loss of internal balance.

Another important reason for making peace with yourself first is that it will enable you to make peace with others more easily and more realistically. Additionally, if you make peace with yourself, then peace with others is not a prerequisite to your own growth. The adult child who is able to achieve inner peace will be able to break the pattern of having his or her life controlled by others and be able to achieve a viable sense of self-power and control over his or her journey towards recovery. Making peace with others in your life always should be in addition to, never in lieu of, making peace with yourself.

Making Peace With Your Past

Part of making peace with yourself will depend upon your ability to make peace with your emotions about the past. As indicated in Chapter Three, this will require awareness and acceptance of your past. Once this is recognized, however, awareness will need to lead in order to change. For example, making peace with your past often requires confronting your memories, but the goal is not to remember; the goal is to make peace with the accompanying emotions. If you accept these emotions, you will gain control of them, rather than have them continue to control you as they have done since you were a child.

If you allow your memories and emotions to continue to overwhelm you, your past will continue to dominate you today. Although making peace with your past is a prerequisite to making peace with yourself, your ability to make peace with yourself is the *most* important aspect of recovery. It will dominate all other phases, but once achieved, you will no longer be vulnerable to domination by others.

True peace for the adult child is achieved by learning to know yourself and learning that you have the power to accept and change yourself. You are the keeper of your own inner peace.

Looking At Yourself

Do you like yourself? What do you like or not like? Can you sit down and make a list of your positive and negative traits? Do you want to change and if so, what do you want to change about yourself?

All of these are powerful questions which can be asked when attempting to establish a realistic perception of yourself. However, before attempting recovery, the adult child will need to assess not only what he or she is trying to recover from, but also the direction of change to be pursued. Not all adult children will assess themselves the same, and not all of the adult child will need to be changed. Each adult child will need to recognize his or her positive characteristics. Try sitting down right now and making small lists by answering the following questions.

What three things are you good at?

What three personality characteristics do you possess of which you are proud?

What three things do you think others like about you?

Now do the same exercise, but list your dislikes in each of the three categories.

As simple as this exercise is, you will need to do it over and over again mentally in order to establish and maintain a realistic assessment of your competence, your deficiencies, and your positive and negative personality characteristics.

Another place to begin self-assessment is to refer to your scores on the personality characteristics found in Chapter One. Several issues should start to become clearer to you as you develop a better picture of yourself. One is that you do possess qualities you should retain. It does not matter that you had to develop these qualities under negative situations; it matters only that you recognize them and use them today. Second, you will need to assess which characteristics you would like to change, which ones you want to abandon entirely and which ones you would like to develop. Third, it is obvious there is a great difference between wanting to change and actually changing.

Progressing from awareness of self to changing is a process which requires energy. Awareness does not guarantee change, but it can stimulate the desire. On the other hand, raising one's level of awareness and not acting on it can increase one's level of frustration, since one is now even more aware of the need to change. Either way, awareness of your behaviors and personality characterisitics will help to establish a foundation upon which you can assess which changes are needed, which directions are indicated and which current characteristics can facilitate these processess. This process can start with assessing how you adapted to parental alcoholism and how this has contributed to who you are today.

Assessing Your Adaptive Behaviors

Much of making peace with yourself will be dependent upon understanding why you behave the way you do. Often, bringing about self-change means changing your motivations. For many adult children of alcoholics, their motivations may have their origin in the adaptive patterns learned through parental alcoholism. Although many children from dysfunctional families share similar behaviors, what causes them to differ are not their behaviors but rather their motivations for the behaviors.

For example, emerging from an alcoholic family with a strong need to be in control may have been motivated by wanting to reduce the anxiety associated with chaos by assuming control over situations. Among children who suffered from parental neglect, it may have developed because of the inability of others to meet their physical needs, thus these children took control in order to survive physically. The adult child who wants to understand better can begin by examining which behaviors today are largely patterns they developed in childhood. Additionally, understanding the motivations may help the adult child to accept his or her behaviors.

The key to surviving an alcoholic family is adaptation. However, this adaptation does not occur in only one area of behavior and it does not develop in a short time. Usually the adaptation involves a collection of behaviors which form patterns that are repeated. Many alcoholic families become "habit cages" where individuals become locked into behaviors because of their constant reacting to alcoholism. Thus, what emerges for many children are clusters of behaviors which eventually are adaptive patterns that become part of the individual behaviors. It is highly likely, therefore, many of these patterns developed in childhood will be continued in adulthood, unless the adult is cognitively able to alter the patterns.

These adaptive patterns have been identified by other names, such as master status roles, family norms or typologies. For example, it has been stated frequently that children of alcoholics disproportionately fall into specific "roles" in the alcoholic family. These childhood roles raise some interesting questions.

From where did they come? What behaviors are identified with each one, and are children of alcoholics the only ones to possess these behaviors? Are they carried into adulthood? How does one abandon childhood roles? Can a person possess more than one role? Are these roles valid?

To answer some of these questions, it is necessary to get a better understanding of the origins, the positive and negative implications, and the limitations of these adaptive patterns known as roles.

Initially, these roles were developed by examining how children in dysfunctional families responded. The early work of Nathan Ackerman in the development of family therapy identified two roles which were believed to be characteristic of children in dysfunctional families. These roles were "hero" and "scapegoat"(Ackerman, 1958). Virginia Satir added to these the roles of "lost child" and "mascot" from her work in family therapy (Satir, 1972). What is similar to both of these family therapists is that they developed these roles to fit children in dysfunctional families. These roles were not initially identified with a specific form of a dysfunctional family. Additionally, it was believed that possessing of each of these roles was correlated with ordinal position and that the oldest child would be associated disproportionately with being a hero, the second child with being a scapegoat, the third with being the lost child, and the youngest child with being the family mascot.

Sharon Wegscheider-Cruse studied these roles and believed that they were also applicable to children of alcoholics. It is important to understand that these roles did not describe children from alcoholic homes only, but indicated that children of alcoholics are children from dysfunctional families. Additionally, adding birth order to each role makes it very possible that some of the behaviors in each role can be found in all children of a similar birth order. For example, eldest children in a family typically have duties and responsibilities the younger children do not, and as a result it should not be surprising to find a characteristic of responsibility in not only eldest children of dysfunctional families, but in eldest children in general. There have been many variations and discussions of these four roles, but typically they have dominated much of the early theoretical or clinical observations about children of alcoholics. However, these roles have their positive as well as negative outcomes. On the one hand, they have helped to provide a category for a clustering of behaviors and have helped many people understand the behaviors of children in alcoholic families. Utilized in this application, they have been helpful.

When they have been applied solely to children of alcoholics, however, they have undermined, alcoholized or caused to be ignored what can be learned from all dysfunctional families in order to help all children. Children of alcoholics do not have a corner on the market on dysfunctional families. To the extent that these roles have helped to provide better insight, they have been positive, but when the roles have been used to predict future behavior, they have become restrictive. It is as if the adult child must say, "Because I adapted this way as a child, I will always adapt to future situations the same way." Other restrictions could include accepting that there are only four possible adaptive patterns. In this chapter we will discuss at least eight possible patterns.

Finally, the most severe restriction is when these roles are interpreted as mutually exclusive patterns, that is, that the child adapts to and possesses only one of these roles. Children of alcoholics, as well as children reared in other dysfunctional families, possess all of these roles simultaneously. At different developmental times in their lives they may identify more with one role than with the others, but they will still possess some of the characteristics of each. These roles represent a typology, on an ideal type. They are not absolutes, but rather representative of patterns of behavior that disproportionately were developed because of adaptive responses.

Since an individual may adapt in a variety of ways to a situation, it is possible he or she will possess a combination of these typologies, with the possibility that one or more patterns is dominant for a while. Although typically they are developed in childhood, there is a high probability that many CoAs carry them into adulthood.

What are the characteristics of these patterns when found in adults and, more importantly for the adult child who wants to make peace with himself or herself, how does one abandon unwanted childhood roles? The following discussion will examine the characteristics of eight of these patterns of behaviors carried into adulthood, keeping in mind several factors.

1. Not all adult children can be found in any one or a combination of these eight.
2. If they do exist in an adult child, they will be found in combinations rather than alone.

3. Not all parts of a typology or role are negative. Some of the characteristics of a given role may in fact be very functional, and it is only the degree to which a role can be possessed that raises possible negative implications.
4. Most important, these roles can be changed, abandoned or restructured to provide assets rather than remaining liabilities only. Remember, if the majority of adult children are survivors, how could they be dominated by roles that are totally negative?

Adaptive Behavior Pattern 1: Hero

Behaviors often associated with the hero pattern include high levels of responsibility, the need for many accomplishments, overly controlling, leadership qualities, perfectionism and the need to be wholly competent. Children with "heroitis" in alcoholic families are often referred to as "junior parents" because of their exceptional levels of competency and their ability to assist others. If they are identified disproportionately with behaviors which are adult-like, as children, what is an adult child hero? An adult child hero is one who still is locked into the same behaviors but under different circumstances.

The child who adapts to many of the hero behavior patterns does so because of an adaptive response to an unhealthy situation. The adult child who continues the behaviors, even though removed from this situation, has internalized the patterns and unable to change. The emotional motivation for both the child and adult hero are the same. Heroes are usually very accomplishment oriented. They need and, in fact, have very high levels of accomplishments. These accomplishments bring recognition from others, which provides validation one has done well. It is not the validation of the accomplishment that is so important for the hero, but the recognition of accomplishments which, in turn, validates self-worth for the hero. Although the hero is exceptionally competent behaviorally, an underlying feeling of inadequacy, which pushes the hero to seek acceptance, is the driving force for the hero.

In their minds, if you accept the accomplishments, you accept the performers. If the accomplishment is worthy, so is the person. Thus, what may separate the child hero from the adult hero is the size of the accomplishment, with the adult child having to continually out-perform himself or herself. Each accomplishment brings validation, but it is never enough because the validation of self-worth is always externally provided. The adult child who is a hero must be able to achieve a personal sense of adequacy and self-worth which can be internally validated and maintained. Otherwise the adult child is very similar to the driven personality person described earlier by Baldwin (1985) with the problem of, "If I am what I do, then who am I if I don't?".

For many adult children being a hero is another mixed message. To others they appear extremely competent and to themselves they feel less than adequate, worthwhile only when they are doing something worthwhile. How does the hero stay at the emotional top without pushing himself or herself to be the best? The adult hero who has an exceptional case of heroitis has a limited perception of numerical success. There is only one acceptable emotional temporary position for the adult hero — first place. It is an all or nothing position that reflects the need for perfectionism; anything less brings emotional inadequacy. It is a lonely place.

The adult child who is a hero and wants to change will need to consider several issues. First, not all behaviors associated with being a hero are negative. What is so wrong with being competent, responsible or occupationally successful? Unless these behaviors impede your ability to grow, there is nothing wrong with them, but you will need to separate those parts of being a hero that are assets from those that are liabilities. The assets will need to be put into perspective, and the liabilities will need to be changed. The hero will need to come to the realization he or she is more than the sum of his or her accomplishments.

Realizing this, however, will not be easy because the hero will be making the transition from external worth to internal worth. This may require altering personal criteria of competent behavior. The hero will need to accept that he or she does not need to be the best all the time, that being wrong is not only normal but also acceptable, and that there are other ways to receive recognition than through his/her accomplishments or those of others. The hero who is able to provide an internal sense of self-worth, to say that he or she possesses many qualities, not just quantities of accomplishments, and to accept the limitations of being normal eventually will be well on the way to releasing the negative patterns found in this typology. The hero must realize that he or she does not own all of the responsibilities that are self-imposed, that choices are available and that being the best at accomplishments does not mean he or she is the best they can be. Competence and the ability to excel should be in addition to, not in lieu of, who you are.

Adaptive Behavior Pattern 2: The Scapegoat

This adaptive pattern consists of such behaviors as internalizing the family chaos and externalizing it through inappropriate behaviors, acting out, high levels of anger, blaming and high levels of visibility. The scapegoat child often is the most visible child of the alcoholic, not because of the alcoholism, but because of the child's behavior. Unfortunately, most scapegoats develop into such because they become easy targets for the family chaos that exists.

For example, many spouses in an alcoholic situation begin to focus on the difficulties of the child, rather than confront the alcoholism or the marital difficulties. Thus the child picks up such messages as "If you were not in trouble all of the time, there would not be so much turmoil in this family." The exact opposite may be true but the scapegoats now find themselves behaving in patterns that do in fact keep them in trouble, in self-destructive episodes, or being blamed not only for their own troubles, but also for others as well.

Scapegoats often become the focus of attention in the family so others can avoid focusing on the real causal and underlying issues. This pattern can be carried into adulthood, but may be even more problematic for the adult scapegoat due to the fact that the inappropriate behavior may now have even more serious consequences. Often the emotional motivation for adult scapegoats is underlying anger and resentment, usually associated with childhood experiences.

Releasing this anger or resentment is likely to increase the visibility of the scapegoat, even though underlying feelings are unnoticed, because he or she was the external focus of someone else's feelings. Just as the behavior of the scapegoat may have been secondary to family issues, the release of anger and resentment by the adult child may be a secondary effort to bring attention to more serious personal issues.

Unfortunately, most adult scapegoats get little attention until they engage in behavior that is wholly inappropriate. As a child it did not take much inappropriate behavior to be recognized, but as the child grew so did the size of the inappropriate behavior needed to draw attention.

Making peace for the adult scapegoat will require accepting that, like it or not, he or she may be engaging in socially inappropriate behavior for which he or she will be held accountable. If the scapegoat uses the fact that he or she is an adult child of an alcoholic as an excuse not to accept responsibility for his or her behavior, the adult child likely will be engaging in the same rationalization the alcoholic parent used. The adult scapegoat must be able to separate the behavior from the real cause. Inappropriate behavior will not bring appropriate intervention; it will add to the problems for the adult child, and it will postpone self-peace.

The adult scapegoat will need to work through feelings of anger and resentment, so as not to employ the same interaction patterns with others and to find socially acceptable behaviors for handling feelings. What is particularly critical for adult scapegoats is that although they were blamed by others, they will not be able to blame others for their situation.

Adult scapegoats who want to abandon their role will need to work through the feelings of being externally controlled by others and thus will need to stop externally focusing the source of their problems. Working through the feelings of anger and resentment that are other-directed may allow the scapegoat to release the same feelings.

For the adult scapegoat making peace with yourself will require the release of the most threatening feeling to achieving inner peace — anger.

Adaptive Behavior Pattern 3: The Lost Child

Unlike most of the other adaptive patterns which are more readily identifiable, the lost child pattern is much more difficult to assess. The distinguishing features for the lost child are that his or her behaviors are not obviously apparent. Those who adapted to this pattern as children are the ones who were emotionally lost in their own families. They get lost in the chaos.

The behaviors most often associated with these children are that they are withdrawn, emotionally isolated, shy, extremely quiet, avoid pressures and are insecure and powerless.

The lost child in the family attempts to avoid any conflict and involvement if possible. Unfortunately, they achieve this at the expense of independence, assertiveness and a sense of belonging. The emotional motivation for the lost child pattern is usually a feeling of relative unimportance. This opinion is carried into adulthood, and the adult lost child continues to be dominated by feelings of deference to everyone. An adult lost child reacts to anyone and everyone, because adult lost children put themselves second in all situations or consider their own needs so unimportant as not even to be mentioned. Therefore, the adult lost child is the most difficult to identify.

These adults attempt to go through life avoiding contact situations, yet they hate to be alone for fear of abandonment. A typical statement by an adult lost child is "If you knew all about me, you wouldn't like me". The adult lost child feels overshadowed by life views in perspective as being part of "that family", rather than as an individual with a separate identity. This lack of identity may result from the stance of passive resistance many adult lost children adopt to survive. They attempt to be the spectators in life, but unfortunately living in an alcoholic family is not a spectator event. To one degree or another, everyone is involved. The adult lost child adapts by developing the patterns of least resistance.

The adult lost children who want to change will be faced with several issues. Initially the adults must realize they possess positive behaviors. They are probably very creative, extremely flexible and have low levels of gratification. In intervention, however, they usually are dominated by their other patterns. Change for the lost child must be more carefully approached and not attempted in large increments.

Traditionally, adult lost children do not respond well in groups because they try to get lost. This is particularly so if there is a hero in the group to offer them protection. The adult lost children will need to understand that their patterns of behavior are the very ones that keep them isolated and powerless — perhaps the very issues that brought them into intervention in the first place.

To recover, the adult lost children will need to abandon the feelings of helplessness and passive resistance.

Adult lost children will need to achieve a healthy sense of self-importance and acknowledge that not only do they have rights, but that these rights are normal. Adult lost children must realize that they can influence their own lives directly and that their lives are not a rehearsal for the real thing but are the real thing itself.

Adaptive Behavior Pattern 4: The Mascot

The adaptive behaviors in this pattern include manipulation, suppression, immaturity, stress avoidance, anxiety and overdependence. The mascot child is usually the youngest family member and for many reasons engages in behaviors that attempt to portray the exact opposite of the family situation. These behaviors appear to be motivated externally and then internally adopted by the mascot child.

Externally their origins may be found in the behaviors of other family members who attempt to protect the youngest child from family tension, alcoholism and dysfunctional behaviors. The child becomes something to protect and then observed for signs that the protection is working by looking for behaviors that are the opposite of the family tension.

Internally, the mascot begins to realize what is expected and begins to act in ways that will meet these expectations. In childhood this usually means exhibiting a jovial carefree attitude, even about the most serious situation. The mascot may be the family jester on demand or "our one shining star". However, the protectionist behaviors of others may develop an unhealthy sense of dependency in this child and a high level of anxiety about the ability to alleviate stressful situations.

The emotional motivations for the mascot children may be fear of exposure and abandonment. That is, they portray the exact opposite of reality and do not want it or themselves exposed. Additionally, abandonment may be disproportionately feared because of the child's development of an inappropriate sense of dependency. Adult mascots retain these emotional motivations, but their behaviors may expand beyond their felt need to alleviate tension for themselves and others by way of entertainment.

Some adult mascots may feel they are the ones who are expected to represent their families positively. Now that they are adults, immaturity and excessive humor are no longer appropriate. Therefore, they engage in behaviors they feel others want them to exhibit in order to represent the family positively.

For example, since the youngest supposedly was protected, the youngest should not have been affected, showing any signs of effect would be unacceptable. Although the family members may have given up on themselves or their own situation, they may feel relieved that "at least the mascot will make it". This puts tremendous pressure on the adult mascots and may lead to the feeling that he or she does everything to fulfill everyone else's expectations but nothing to fulfill his or her own. This is very similar to their childhood predicament. They did not cause the family stress, but felt responsible to relieve it.

Many adult mascots may feel externally programmed by the expectations to alleviate others' pain and stress and at the same time to display none themselves. Adult mascots in recovery will need to realize that not all of their patterns are negative. They possess many positive characteristics to facilitate recovery. For example, having a sense of humor, having a sense of obligation to others and not taking things too seriously can all aid in recovery, if not carried to extremes.

In recovery the adult mascots must learn to control behavior that may be distracting, such as laughing inappropriately, not assessing the seriousness of their own or others' situations and tending to alleviate tension rather than allow it to be processed.

Adult mascots must abandon the limited self-identity of a single response to all situations and allow themselves to develop more fully their potential for alternative behaviors. With a greater repertoire of alternative behaviors and feelings, mascots should be able to more productively represent the most important people in their lives — themselves.

Adaptive Behavior Pattern 5: The Placator

This pattern of behavior was identified by Claudia Black, and its characteristics include conflict avoidance, enabling, over responsiblity and fear (Black, 1982). Children who displayed these patterns were the family counselor, mediator or arbitrator. Unlike others who are professional mediators or arbitrators who intervene after a conflict to attempt a resolution, the placator in the family fears conflict and attempts to avoid it at all costs. Thus they are consistently putting "band aids" on every symptom of trouble in order to minimize conflict, so the source will never be confronted. Confrontation is the enemy of the placator.

The emotional motivation for the placator pattern is conflict avoidance and a desire for family peace. It is a way for children in chaotic situations, who are powerless over the source of chaos, to attempt some control by helping maintain a livable balance. Adult placators may continue the same behaviors of conflict avoidance, even though they are constantly placating conflicts.

It is ironic that the placator in many instances finds himself or herself consistently in situations that need resolution, even though they fear conflict. Do adult placators unknowingly get themselves into crisis situations and then feel that they are responsible for solving them? Do adult placators find themselves in troubled relationships or enter potentially troubled ones because they think they can straighten them out?

The recovering adult placator possesses many potentially positive skills, which usually results in being highly sensitive to others, willing to explore a variety of alternatives to seek a solution, being good at communication and persistent (a "never-give-up" attitude). These can be tremendous assets for the recovering placator if the individual is willing to use them on himself or herself, rather than on other people. This is not to say that the placator is adept enough to be his or her own counselor (not that they haven't tried!), but rather that if kept in perspective, these qualities can become internal strengths, rather than external skills.

One of the major problems for the recovering placator is learning to be able to receive from others. We know that placators are great at giving, but how good are they at receiving? Placators will help everyone else but will not allow anyone to assist them. For some placators this is a form of avoidance. The more they help others, the less they must deal with themselves.

Placators must abandon the patterns that make them feel responsible for solving others' problems. It is also important for the placator to establish a more realistic perception of conflict, to understand that conflict not only is normal between people, but that it can also bring about positive change that otherwise might be avoided. The placator must realize that to continue his or her behavior perpetuates the problems.

The placator must realize that there is a great difference between helping someone and solving their problems. The greatest part of intervention with others is that they no longer need you to intervene. As a placator, you are extremely susceptible to user relationships at the expense of your own fulfillment.

If helping others is such a good idea, then help yourself to your own idea. You cannot help others achieve a viable peace if you have not reached it yourself. Get your act together before you take it on the road.

Adaptive Behavior Pattern 6: Hypermaturity

This pattern of behavior is very different from the others because of the fact that it is not one characterized by behavior but by attitude. The adult child with hypermaturity possesses an attitude of extreme seriousness, not only about himself or herself but about everything he or she does. Unlike the hero pattern, which is dominated by behavioral accomplishments, the hypermature pattern is dominated by thought processes of extreme seriousness, exceptional self-criticism, emotion controlling, and difficulty with the ability to relax or enjoy comfortably.

The hypermature adult child is always mentally on guard, and in many respects is the "eternal parent". The adult is locked into behaviors that will not allow the adult to relax, to release tension, to enjoy himself or others, or to act his age. The person is always emotionally ahead of his physical, chronological development.

In childhood, hypermaturity may not have been recognized by others as a liability, but rather as a positive attitude in the child. For example, the hypermature child may be the child who at age 11 or 12 acts and emotionally feels as if he or she were 21 or 22, or the 15-year-old child who feels the emotional impact of being 30.

What is unfortunate, however, is that these attitudes may be valued by adults, and are not seen as age-inappropriate behaviors, which may have later developmental consequences. The adult who has a childish attitude may be chastised, but the child with an adult-like attitude is praised.

The best time to engage in childish activities is when you are a child. Many adult children, especially those who are hypermature, express feelings in support groups that they feel as if they missed their childhood. Many hypermature adult children do not have a specific issue that has brought them to seek intervention. They merely feel as if something is missing. Why do they feel as if something is missing? Because something *is* missing. Perhaps it is their childhood or perhaps it is an attitude that will free them from extreme maturity.

One sign of hypermaturity is the feeling there is not a specific problem but rather everything in general is problematic; the result is a "burned out" feeling. They are emotionally drained or suffer from "compassion fatigue", which results from being emotionally exhausted to the point they are not able to care or feel to the degree they would like. Such a person in his or her early thirties in a support group appears emotionally burned out. You ask, "How old are you?" and they reply, "Thirty four". You then ask, "How long have you felt like an adult?" and they reply, "About twenty years"!

The hypermature adult child possesses mental attitudes about responsibility and serious emotions which may have served some positive adaptive functions for the young child, but as an adult these attitudes may impede being able to enjoy themselves or others.

Hypermature adult children may be exceptional parents quantitatively, but have difficulty qualitatively interacting with their children. They are not able to let the child in themselves meet the emotions of the child they are parenting.

Hypermature adult children must remember, while their own childhood may be over, its emotions are still available. Hypermature children may personify in exaggerated forms the characteristics of taking themselves very seriously and judging themselves without mercy which are found in many adult children, as discussed in Chapters One and Two. What separates those who are dominated by hypermature patterns from the other adaptive patterns is that the hypermature adult children are more extreme in possessing these characterisitics. The major emotional motivation for the hypermature individual is maintaining control over his or her emotions, often at the expenses of denying them.

The adult child with hypermaturity who wants to change his or her emotional attitudes will need to begin to reduce the unnecessary feelings of responsibility and seriousness. One of the best indicators of recovery is the development of a healthy sense of humor. The hypermature adult child will need to reduce the degree of importance to events, because the hypermature adult child attaches unrealistic levels of importance to average events. Such an adult child lacks a normal perspective on normal events.

For example, hypermature adult children will need to stop giving everything top priority. In their estimation everything is incredibly important, deserves top priority, and needs to be done now. With this kind of attitude, is it any wonder that the hypermature person feels overwhelmed and emotionally drained? Breaking this cycle will require breaking the method in which one approaches not only tasks, but also the attitude about those tasks.

Even though it is simplistic, one must say to them : "Quit taking yourself so seriously. You still can take what you *do* seriously, keeping it in perspective, but stop taking *yourself* so seriously. Contrary to popular belief, your attitudes about the world are not the highest point of attitudinal evolution. So, take it easy. Angels can fly because they take themselves lightly. The sun will not set any earlier because you have passed this way earlier. Learn to keep yourself and your tasks in perspective. Laughter, warmth, enjoyment and self contentment should be part of every age of development, so relax and act your age."

Adaptive Behavior Pattern 7: The Detacher

This is a response behavior by the adult child to disengage emotionally and psychologically from people and situations which the adult child considers undesirable. It is characterized by premature closure, denial and a desire not to be emotionally vulnerable. The emotional motivation is to avoid being hurt by becoming non-feeling or emotionally numb.

Detaching from a situation can be either a healthy or

unhealthy response. For some adult children of alcoholics, detaching may have been a healthy response to an unhealthy situation. For others, detaching may be an unhealthy behavior used to avoid dealing with any undesirable situation. Thus the motivations and procedures in detaching become more critical than the actual behavior.

Most detachment for adult children who fit this pattern begins in adolescence. At age 15 the adolescent perceives that not only is the family extremely chaotic, but from now on he or she will no longer allow the situation to bother him or her. The adolescent thus tries to detach emotionally from the situation in which he or she is living. Is the adolescent's detachment a healthy response to an unhealthy situation (the adolescent feels a need to be in a healthy environment), or is it establishing a pattern whereby any and all uncomfortable situations will be abandoned quickly?

Although there is no such thing as a healthy alcoholic situation, detaching from it emotionally can be at least a temporary solution, detachment may have significant effects later for the adult child. It can inhibit the adult child from working through negative feelings about being reared in an alcoholic home, because the adult believes that he or she succeeded in detaching from the situation so why should there be any "leftover" emotional baggage?

The adult child may be caught in an emotional trap. If the detachment was successful, there would be no feelings from the past, but if the feelings persist, does that mean that the detachment was not successful? This can be further complicated if the detacher actually believes that he or she totally disengaged.

Detachment is never total. Although you may physically leave a situation, it will remain with you emotionally until you can gradually let go of these emotions. Some detachers will be proud of the fact they were able to separate themselves and believe they have no ill effects from the experience. For them, acknowledging any effects is a threat to their detachment. Adult children who have detached in this manner will need to understand that the feelings from the past are not only normal, but also that they will need to be worked through for the detachment to be healthy.

Another problem associated with detachment is "premature closure". This occurs when the adult child, who is faced with any uncomfortable situation, decides to leave it rather than to attempt resolution. Premature closure occurs when a person in a relationship or situation experiences a problem and perceives that the only solution is to leave. The individual does not consider alternatives or working through problems. All solutions are the same — leave. Thus the person not only leaves a situation too early, but also does not develop problem-solving skills.

For example, at the first indication of trouble in a relationship the person wants out. A good relationship is perceived only as totally trouble-free, and any problems indicate that it is time to be abandoned. This adult child may jump from relationship to relationship looking for the ideal one, never recognizing that his or her concept of a good relationship is not real. Healthy relationships require interaction and work, not abandonment.

Finally, the detacher, like all children of alcoholics, is confronted with overcoming denial. For detachers this may be even more difficult because in order to overcome denial, they may have to face their own motivations for detachment. Detachers do not want to feel vulnerable to anyone or any situation. Their denial of parental alcoholism is also a denial of there being any effects. Not being able to detach, means they are vulnerable. It should come as no surprise that few detachers are found in adult childrens' groups. Of all the adaptive behaviors, this one may be the hardest to reach. It may be necessary for the detacher to explore the feelings associated with vulnerability and denial first, before addressing the parental alcoholism.

The adult child who believes that he or she is detached from the alcoholic situation will need to examine several issues. First, was the reason for the detachment healthy or unhealthy? Has detachment become a way of handling all undesirable relationships or situations? Does the adult child possess the abilities to resolve conflict? Certainly knowing when to disengage yourself from a negative situation is beneficial. In fact, some adult children suffer from just the opposite. They stay too long and eventually feel trapped. The detacher will need to develop a healthy balance in assessing situations and not be guided by an all-or-nothing approach.

Adaptive Behavior Pattern 8: The Invulnerable

Is it possible to come from an alcoholic family and be a healthy adult? *Yes.* Research indicates that some children from highly dysfunctional families can emerge as healthy adults without intervention (Garmezy, 1976). Invulnerable means that the adult child possesses certain characterisitics that have allowed them to live through an experience without denying it and still maintain a healthy sense of balance and development. Invulnerable does not mean the adult child was not affected or that nothing can harm him or her. There are times when the invulnerable is vulnerable.

What may separate the invulnerable from the hero or hypermature pattern, however, is that the truly invulnerable person not only will admit when he or she is vulnerable, but also will act to reduce the stress. Heroes and hypermatures usually do not want to admit vulnerablity because it is feared as a weakness.

There are two kinds of invulnerable behavior patterns which can be associated with adult children of alcoholics. One developed during childhood and allowed the child to emerge as a healthy adult. The second is developed in adulthood and allows the adult child to overcome a negative childhood. In the first type, the ability to become invulnerable is dependent upon many factors such as those mentioned in Chapter Two. An additional factor, however, is related to the personality type of the child. Is the glass half empty or half full?

E. E. Werner points out that some children are more resilient to stress in the alcoholic family (Werner, 1986). The personality of the child may help to develop attitudes about the alcoholism in the family to manage the situation. Some adult children who are less affected by parental alcoholism may attribute this more to themselves than to any other offsetting factor. They were not the type of persons to be easily discouraged or depressed; their basic disposition became an asset.

Another consideration is that they possess a certain degree of "invulnerability". This may be found more in the second type of invulnerable, which allows the adult child in adulthood to overcome a negative childhood. Adaptive patterns of behavior are not unrelated categories, but rather occur in combinations. Therefore, what makes many adult children of alcoholics survivors may be the degree of invulnerability that was combined with their other adaptive behaviors. Just as I think all adult children of alcoholics will possess some characteristics of all eight of these patterns, I think that some degree of invulnerableness will be found in each pattern.

If an adult child overly identifies with one or two of the adaptive patterns, but wants to outgrow any of the negative aspects, it is possible he or she will want to grow into the adaptive pattern of being invulnerable. The invulnerable adult child is a healthy adult. He or she has been able to make the transition fully from a negative childhood into a functional healthy adult. The invulnerable adult child is an adult child well into recovery. He or she is now capable of all of the potential has been underdeveloped. He or she is able to turn the liabilities of childhood into adult assets. The invulnerable adult is able to let go and grow by letting go and growing at the same time. Invulnerability, although facilitated by personality, is learned. The invulnerable adult allows himself or herself to grow from all experiences, negative as well as positive. This adult never loses his or her ability to hope, to risk, to try, to forgive, to go beyond injury, to share and to love.

These eight adaptive pattern behaviors represent some of the typologies found among adult children of alcoholics. It is possible that they are found to some degree among all adults and in adults from other forms of dysfunctional families. Each typology has positive and negative consequences, and it is not uncommon for an adult child to possess more than one of these patterns. As the adult child looks back on life it is possible that at different ages he or she identified with one or more different patterns than now. At different ages, different adaptive patterns may have been used, or perhaps the same combination of patterns has persisted. Additionally, the different ways in which we all learn, our cognitive learning processes, may have affected not only how the different patterns developed, but also which patterns developed. A good example of this diversity is in the following vignette in which Sharon, an adult daughter of an alcoholic father, shares her insights.

SHARON'S STORY

Before I became "chemically free", my life as a child, then as a wife and mother, in Los Angeles, and later in Pennsylvania, was going nowhere.

My life was such a disaster, you wouldn't believe it. I prayed to die, I begged to die. I attempted suicide many times, to no avail. I finally decided the only thing I was good at was failing.

Today I realize I'm a fighter; I'm a survivor. I truly wanted to live but I just didn't know how. I was afraid.

Because of my past and all the pain I have experienced, I am able to work with newly recovering persons today. When I get the opportunity, I also speak at schools and other organizations. I want to let people everywhere know there is hope. No matter how hopeless or helpless they feel, there is hope and there is help.

Both drugs and alcohol caused problems in my life. I was introduced to drugs very early in my life. I was eight years old.

At age six, I was raped by one of my uncles. As far back as I can remember, I was sexually abused by my alcoholic father. Many years later I found out that my older sister was also sexually abused by our father. My uncle and father both threatened me, "Be silent or else." As a result I developed a hatred of sex. I thought it was dirty and ugly. Because of my upbringing and the experiences I had, it affected my opinion of men. I told my mother about my father but she called me a liar.

My father, who had been admitted at one time to a mental institution, would beat my older sister and I with a "razor strap", for suspected or minor transgressions. If my mother said we had been bad, we got a beating. If he thought we had been bad, we got a beating. There were times we didn't do anything but got a beating anyway.

At the age of six, I saw my first psychiatrist. By age eight, pain pills were prescribed. The doctor said I was having migraine headaches. I now know it was stress I didn't know how to deal with. By age ten I was diagnosed as having a nervous breakdown. Tranquilizers were prescribed.

At this time we moved. My parents bought a house in a different city. Moving didn't make anything better. I had failed the 5th grade, which wasn't my fault. I was very much underweight (I only weighed 50 pounds at age ten) and I was acutely anemic, so I was constantly under the doctors care.

Because of this I was unable to keep up with all the school work.
So I was failed.

When we moved, I repeated the fifth grade again. Shortly
after starting school, I realized the work was far too easy. I
asked my mother to go to school and talk to the principle about
moving me ahead to the sixth grade. She said she couldn't do
that. I told her to have them test me to see if I could function in
the sixth grade, but she told me no. As a result, I lost all my study
skills and all interest in school. Life was a total waste to me.

This is when I made my first suicide attempt. I strangled
myself with a scarf. Somewhere between passing out and dying,
I loosened the scarf. From that point on, there were many more
suicide attempts and many more psychiatrists.

Until recently, I never leveled with the psychiatrists. Not
because I didn't want to, but because I didn't know what was
causing me all my problems. I never mentioned about being
raped or being sexually abused because I knew if I ever said
anything, I would be punished worse than I had ever been
punished. As I grew older, I couldn't say anything because I felt
dirty and ugly and guilty.

Happiness in my childhood was rare. I did get involved in
Square Dancing. I really enjoyed it. I could dance, have a good
time and no one was putting me down. I seemed to pick up the
dancing very easily. I practiced a lot. I had to be the best one
there. I worked very hard to be the best.

I took one year of accordion lessons when I was nine years
old. After only two lessons, my sister told our parents she
wanted to be in a talent show at our school and wanted me to
accompany her on the accordion, so I took the sheet music to
my teacher and asked him to put a left hand to it, because the
music was for the piano. He told me I couldn't play sheet music
that soon. I told him to put the left hand to it and I would play
it. He did and I did. We came in second place in the talent show.
The night of the show I was running a 103° temperature because
I was coming down with the measles. We still got second place.

My parents praised my sister for such a good performance.
The only thing they said to me was why didn't we get first
place. I should have done better. Around 11 years old, I entered
a yo-yo contest at my school during the summer. I had to
borrow a kid's yo-yo to do the tricks because I didn't have one.
I would stand in line and practice the trick before I was called
on to perform. I had never used a yo-yo before that. I won the
contest. After showing my parents my first place ribbon and

doing a lot of begging, they finally bought me a yo-yo. The next two contests I also won. Nothing much was ever said about any of the contests I won. There was even an article in the newspaper about me and the boy that won first place in the third contest. This didn't seem to thrill my parents very much. The fourth contest, I came in fourth. This is when they commented; I just wasn't good enough.

I continued with my dancing. As a young teenager we did several personal appearances. We were even on television. We also made a movie, "Country Music Jamboree". This is when we were introduced to acrobatic square dancing. This was a lot of fun. Around 15 years old I started learning other types of dancing. We did a couple of shows for the U.S.O. in Oceanside, California. I was offered a tour overseas, but my mother said no.

I was told all my life how stupid I was. No matter how hard I tried or how good I did, it just wasn't good enough.

I quit playing my accordion, because my father was always bugging me. He wanted me to learn to play without music. He wanted me to sound out everything. He didn't want me using music of any kind. He didn't know how to read music, so he didn't want me using it.

Every time I would get my accordion out to practice, he would be there with his guitar. He wouldn't let me practice my music; he wanted me to play the things he knew. He would yell at me constantly. He would tell me how stupid I was because I couldn't sound out music like he did. Finally I just quit playing. Now I don't even know how to play. The only one I hurt was me. But you could never have told me that then.

After high school, I rushed into marriage. I got married for all the wrong reasons. The marriage lasted three years. We had one child, a boy. When he was just over a year old, my husband and I separated. I moved in with my sister and her family. Of course, I had my son with me. A few months later my husband filed for a divorce. I went to a lawyer and asked what I should do. He told me my choice was to contest or cross-file. So I cross-filed. My mistake. In the meantime my husband got a vacation from his job and asked if he could have our son for a few days. I said O.K., because I felt he should have time with him also. Well, he sure had time with him — for the next 15 years.

While he had him for the couple of days, he ran away with him. I called the police but they told me they couldn't do anything because we hadn't been to court yet for custody. I called my lawyer. He wrote letters to all of my husband's relatives but of course no one had seen or heard anything from him.

I got the divorce on default, because he didn't show up for the hearing. But I lost a son over it. I felt my life was over. My son was all I had. He was the only thing that meant anything to me and now that he was gone, there was no reason for me to live. I tried every way I could think of to die, with no success. I even headed for the freeway one night because that's where the fastest cars were. But I was rescued in spite of myself.

Fifteen years later I received a phone call from my sister. She told me my ex-husband was trying to get in touch with me. She gave me his phone number. I asked her what my ex-husband wanted. She told me. It seems my son wasn't as happy and well adjusted as I had been told he was. December 27, 1981, my son turned 17 years old. He also died December 27, 1981. He hung himself. His half-sister is the one who found him. She was only about six years old.

I called him the next day. He asked me if I would please come out to California for the funeral. I told him I would be there. And I was. After 15 years, I saw my son lying in a casket. Thank God, I had been chemically free for three years when I received the news because I needed every single day of that three years to get me through. I am so grateful to my Higher Power, whom I choose to call God, and all the great friends I have because that is what gave me the strength I needed to see me through.

In August, 1969, I married again. He was from Pennsylvania, but was living in California with his mother. We lived together for a while, but when I got pregnant, I insisted we get married. So we did. Again for all the wrong reasons. We fought like cat and dog all the time, even when we were just living together, but we got married anyway. I was sure having the baby would make everything fine. It didn't. My daughter was born two months later. She was beautiful. I loved her very much, but she couldn't take the place of my son. I still love her very much today. Eighteen months after she was born, I had another child. This time I had another son.

I had been taking a good many pills and drinking during my second pregnancy due to a great deal of stress and sickness.

My husband had been in a shooting accident on a hunting trip with two of his cousins. He came back from the hospital in a full spica body cast. He was completely bedridden for six months and semi-mobile for three months after that.

He had been in the hospital for about six weeks when I found out I was three months pregnant with our second child. I had a lot of problems with this pregnancy. I had a daughter that was one year old, a husband completely bedridden and was pregnant, all at the same time. No one would help me. None of his family or my family ever offered to help in any way. I was finally forced to go to welfare for financial help. I got very sick when I was about five months pregnant, and was taken to the hospital by ambulance. I had an acute case of bronchitis. The very next day when they realized I had no insurance, they released me and sent me home and told me to admit myself to the county hospital. I was unable to do this because the hospital was overflowing, and I had no one to take care of my daughter and husband.

Because my baby was so small, the doctors forced me to carry him for eleven months. When he was finally born, he still only weighed 4.5 pounds. Then my problems really began.

My husband was completely disabled, and soon after my son was born, I started realizing there was something wrong with him. The older he got, the worse things got. I found out my son was multi-handicapped. He is deaf, has motor damage, is hyperactive and has either allergic or reverse reaction to almost every medication on the market. He started having seizures when he was six months old. He finally started sitting alone when he was about ten months old. He took his first step alone when he was 2.5 years old.

When my daughter was in the third grade, they found she had learning disabilities. She has been in special classes ever since then. These classes have helped a great deal. This year coming, she will be in the 11th grade, and she will only be in one special class.

I moved to Pennsylvania ten years ago, after several years of coaxing from my husband. When I first moved to Pennsylvania, I hated it. I had many adjustments to make. For example, I had never seen a live cow before, and the first place I lived, they were my neighbors. I had never seen snow before either. I didn't know what people meant when they said it was calling for "freezing rain", but I soon found out.

I had a rough time getting proper schooling for my deaf son. People just didn't seem to understand the importance of early education for a deaf child. It was even more important in my son's case because of his combination of handicaps. It took me two years to finally get him into a deaf school. I have had to fight with professional people in every area ever since my son was born.

One year after I moved to Pennsylvania, I slipped on the ice on my porch steps and cracked a vertabrae in my back. That put me in the hospital for a week. Two months after that, the day I was bringing my son home from the hospital from having his tonsils and adenoids removed, a coal truck pulled out from a stop sign and ran into the side of my car cracking a couple of my ribs. During the week I was in the hospital with the cracked vertabrae, I tried to cut the jugular vein in my neck.

Although I had been drinking and popping pills for several years, I never once thought of my having a drinking or drug problem. I had never heard of anything such as Alcoholics Anonymous or Alcoholism. All I knew was, in April of 1977, I was sure I was losing my mind. I was sure I was going crazy. My therapist took me to see a doctor in Somerset. Thank God, he was able to pick up on what the problem really was. I was detoxed then sent to a rehabilitation program.

For the first time in my life, I did not want to kill myself.

That was a turning point in my life. I learned a lot about alcoholism and drug addiction while I was there.

In July, 1977, I got news my father was dying of cancer. I made arrangements to go to California to see him. I really hoped my father and I could sit down and talk about everything that had happened in the past and maybe he would apologize. I wanted so much to be able to have a real father/daughter relationship before he died. Little did I expect what transpired.

My stepmother and her oldest foster son picked me up from the airport. We went to her and my father's house. I had my daughter with me also. I had made special arrangements for my son to stay with specially trained people.

Sunday morning I was awakened by my father fondling me. I was very angry. I told him to get out of my room. He did leave. I got up quickly and got dressed. We all went to church. My father's church, where he was a deacon. Everyone there told me what a wonderful person my father was, and what a great job he was doing by raising six foster children. It was all I could do to keep my mouth shut.

That afternoon he called my daughter over to sit on his lap. When I saw what was happening, I knew there was no way we were ever going to be able to straighten anything out. I did try to talk to him but all he said was he just didn't understand what had ever happened between us. The very next day I rented a car and got a motel room for my daughter and I. My stepmother was very angry with me. She told me how terrible I was and all my father wanted was to have a little time to be near me before he died.

After being in California three weeks, I got a phone call that my husband had wrapped his pick-up truck around a tree and was in the hospital. So I made arrangements to come home. How he got out of that accident alive, I don't know. The truck was demolished.

When I came home, I continued to go to A.A. meetings but my life was still a mess. I took care of my husband again. He didn't like the changes in me. He told me he would buy anything I wanted, drugs or alcohol if I would just take it. I told him nothing was going to stand in the way of my sobriety.

Several months after that I left him. My children and I moved to Johnstown, Pennsylvania. I was all right for about a month but I wasn't going to any A.A. meetings. I was trying to handle everything myself. It didn't work. I got drunk. It took me about four weeks to come to grips with myself. Once I realized what I was doing to myself, I started back to A.A. meetings and have been there ever since. My sobriety date is October 22, 1978.

My life is still quite confusing most of the time. I have had several operations in the past seven years. My son still has many problems, and my daughter is suffering from being raised in an alcoholic home. But with a clear head I am able to handle most of the problems.

Today I thrive on working with newly recovering persons. I have a boyfriend who is also in the program, and treats me well. I don't know what the future has in store for me but as long as I stay chemically free, I know it will be good.

Today I know drugs and alcohol are not the answer. They are not going to help you deal with anything. I want people to realize there is hope. No matter how bad you have had it, no matter what you have experienced, there is hope and help. One day at a time, with the help of the fellowship and my Higher Power, I can enjoy the life God has saved for me.

I pray that my story will, in some small way, be an inspiration to someone, somewhere, sometime. There is hope and there is help. We don't have to do it alone.

Sharon F.
Johnstown, Pennsylvania

Sharon thinks of herself today as a survivor and a recovering person, but it is obvious from her story that this was not always the case. In fact as a young girl she identified more with being a lost child and was greatly victimized. Sharon was and is more than a lost child, however. She used all eight adaptive patterns of behavior as a daughter of an alcoholic who attempted to cope not only with the alcoholism, but also with the many abuses in her life. She used adaptive patterns at different periods of her life. She is now aware of the positive and negative influences on her today because of her past. Each adaptive behavior has had its positive and negative implications. They were not all negative. Like other children of alcoholics, it is doubtful that Sharon was fully aware of her patterns of behavior, but they were used and maintained, either because they worked, because she had no alternatives or because they seemed to make the most sense at the time. For whatever reasons, each of the eight patterns was used, some more than others.

For example, in the **hero** pattern we can see her needing to be the best, even at games. Later as an adult she feels that it was necessary for her to handle everything herself.

It is obvious that Sharon was very much identified in the **scapegoat** pattern by her parents. The physical beatings and sexual abuse were accompanied with verbal abuse that she was stupid and never good enough. In the scapegoat pattern, her acting out behaviors were attempts at suicide.

Overshadowing her early years was an identification as a **lost child.** Although she tried repeatedly, it was difficult for her to fit in with her family. She indicated that she was always second to her sister and what she was good at was failing, even though she had successes. Finally, she admits that when she did feel stress, she did not know how to deal with it.

There is not a lot of the **mascot** pattern in Sharon. She states that she pretended many times that the problems were not there, particularly no alcohol or drug problems. Additionally, she feels that she could have done better in some of her attempts to please others.

Sharon engages in some **placating** patterns, especially by never mentioning being raped, abused or parental alcoholism. In her second marriage, she thinks that the birth of a baby will make everything fine. Unfortunately, as a placator she was forced to go along with many problematic behaviors.

Her **hypermaturity** is apparent in her attitudes about herself. She states that there was no fun in her childhood (although under the circumstances we can see why), but as an adult she even admits she knew she was only hurting herself and you could not tell her that.

Her attempts at **detachment** are quite obvious. Suicide is the ultimate detachment. Other behaviors in this pattern were divorce, separating from family and moving. Some of her detachment was healthy behavior, however, such as removing her daughter and herself from further contact with the father, when he began sexually molesting his granddaughter.

Finally, we see Sharon operating many times in the **invulnerable** pattern. Certainly she considers herself a survivor, but realizes this alone is not enough. Much of her invulnerability contributed to her survivability. Today, however, it is contributing to her growth. Repeatedly, she states that today she wants to live, that there is hope and that help is available when you are vulnerable.

My admiration for Sharon is high. Here is a daughter of an alcoholic whose life has been touched by almost every problem imaginable, yet today she is full of hope, willing to share herself to help others, and tells us "there is hope and there is help . . . we don't have to do it alone".

Abandoning Childhood Adaptive Behavior Patterns

Many adult children who come into treatment or support groups feel that they must change totally in order to recover. To them this means abandoning their childhood roles or adaptive behaviors. If adaptive behavior patterns have some positive as well as negative implications, however, why totally abandon them? What the adult child in recovery must do is distinguish between the positive and negative aspects of the unique patterns and decide which elements to keep, which to change and which to abandon. This will require an honest appraisal of the many patterns of behavior that you have. If you are not at peace with yourself, it may be due to maintaining patterns of behaviors that you do not like. Part of making peace with yourself may be letting go of the parts that are limiting you or harming you. How do you begin to abandon childhood roles?

The first step in overcoming childhood roles is to understand them better. That is, what does the role do for you? According to Susan Volchok, childhood roles can have both positive and negative implications (Volchok, 1985). In childhood, roles often produced guidelines for you and contributed to your master status role identity. Thus the fulfillment of your role may have helped you in several of the following ways:

a. kept you from being abandoned
b. provided guidelines for acceptable behavior
c. met the expectations of others
d. helped to create balance
e. helped to overcome inconsistency and chaos.

However, role fulfillment may have affected you negatively in the following ways:

a. kept you from being yourself totally
b. impeded developing alternative behaviors
c. affected your self-concept
d. added pressure to comply

The adult child must deal with what to do with his or her roles. Some may choose to do nothing, preferring to live within the shelter of the role. Others may find the roles too confining and want to find ways to go beyond their role identity. To begin this process, the adult child should make an inventory of all of the positive and negative aspects of the roles that he or she fulfills. Then select those elements of you that you wish to keep, improve, change or abandon.

It is important to realize that as a child, your role development was an adaptive response to a situation over which you had no control. You now have a choice about your roles and your development as an adult. You have a choice to do four things with your roles.

    1. You can overcome them. This will involve working through the role; in spite of its earlier limitations or negative aspects, you can learn to function as you would like. For example, the adult child who feels very

much a lost child is able to work through the feelings of relative unimportance, shyness and passive behavior to become an individual with self-worth.

2. You can try to live up to your childhood role. This is the option that traps many adult children. Rather than abandon their childhood roles, even when they are aware of the limitations, they not only carry them into adulthood, they also keep trying to fulfill them. The adult child perceives that he or she is expected to behave according to his or her role label. Once a hero, always a hero. Once a scapegoat, always a scapegoat. In this manner the role is not only fulfilled, but also preserved. For example, what separates the child hero from the adult hero is only the size of the accomplishment. Unfortunately, living up to a childhood role may leave few alternatives for developing other roles for the adult. Thus change and growth are sacrificed for the sake of maintaining an unwanted identity.

3. You can abandon the role. This requires knowing exactly what you want to stop doing and then stopping. Obviously, this is easier said than done. However, there are many adult children who do not choose to maintain the negative roles of childhood and actively seek ways to eliminate them. For example, the detacher decides not to leave every conversation that is challenging or upsetting and begins to try alternative communication skills. The detacher may think, "I used to leave problems immediately, but now I stay to get a better understanding of my alternatives." The behavior of premature closure is abandoned, and new behaviors are adopted.

4. You can learn to outgrow a role. This requires going beyond the limitations of a role in order to create positive change and growth. The boundaries of a particular role will be consistently broken in order to establish new behaviors. Eventually the adult child stops returning to the confines of the role and simply no longer finds the limitations useful. At this point the role has been outgrown, and one hopes the positive aspects of the role are incorporated into the new identity. Outgrowing a role leads to establishing a new identity, and that identity in turn will continue to change. If the adult child can outgrow the childhood role, then he or

she will no longer be developmentally limited and will be able to experience all of his or her adult capabilities.

In order to change your childhood roles, Volchok offers several suggestions in order to facilitate your changes (Volchok, 1985). These are:

1. **Verbal strategies alone do not work well.**

   Saying that you are going to be different or that you are going to change does not mean that you will. Change means changing. To change, you have to do something besides express a desire. Talking may give you insight, doing gives results.

2. **Explore why people see you in your role and why you see yourself in a role.**

   What is it about you that identifies you with a particular behavior pattern? Helping to understand yourself as others perceive you may clarify your roles and allow you to understand more fully what it is that you want to change. Some adult children see themselves as others see them. Other adult children have a totally different opinion of themselves from what others have. Still other adult children are vague about their role identity, either internally or externally. It is important to establish a single, realistic, consistent identity, rather than to attempt to change several without knowing which is the real you.

3. **Demonstrate and live the change.**

   This will require you to be who you want to be now. This involves the actual limiting and abandoning of behaviors you do not like. The practicing of new behaviors must begin, and you must incorporate the positive aspects of the past with the desired new behaviors. For example, if someone accused you of being a recovering adult child, could they find enough evidence to convict you? Think about this: what is it about you that is recovering, what has changed and what do you like now about yourself? Are you beginning to make peace with yourself? The adult child who can answer these questions satisfactorily is at the point where he or she can say, "I am, and I am becoming . . ." one hopes this means that the adult child is becoming the kind of person he or she would like to be at this time in his or her life. However, as discussed in the last suggestion, the "new" you may not be readily accepted by everyone else.

4. **You may have to accept that others will keep their old opinions of you and that you must go on.**

It is not uncommon for adult children of alcoholics who are changing to meet resistance to this change from others. This is especially true from those who may know you the most, those who are threatened by your change, or those who are in need of change themselves. Unfortunately, the best example of this may be found in alcoholic families where rigidity and negative habits are the norm.

Often those who are the most resistant to our changes are those who have known you the longest. In a family, individuals share a common history of their roles. This happens even in the healthiest of families. For example, family members may be labeled the bright one, our little scholar, the athletic one, the funny one, and so forth. Thus family members are used to seeing and interacting with each other not only from the family norms, but also from their expectations of how each member fulfills his or her role.

An adult child who is attempting to change his or her role identity must be prepared to go on, even if others attempt to hold you back or treat you as if you still exist in your old role. Remember, you are not stuck in your old role: they are. You have a choice not to return. I know that when you visit, they may pull your negative strings or sing the same old songs. You have a choice, however. You do not have to sing and dance unless you want to. Remember, you are recovering and changing for yourself, not for your family. You can find new ways, even if others stay in their old ones. Yes, it would be much easier to change if your entire family changed as well, but their growth can no longer be a prerequisite for yours. Others may keep their old opinions or role expectations of you, but you can go on.

5. **You may meet resistance to the new you — go on anyway.**

This problem is similar to others keeping their role expectations of you, but now that you are demonstrating the change, they actively resist it. This may be for a variety of reasons, including their discomfort around you because you are doing now what they would like to do and lack the courage to do. It is possible that by resisting your change, they are in fact resisting their own.

Part of your role change must include the ability to no longer be excessively directed by others. You must be able to abandon childhood roles, even in the face of resistance. If you do not, those roles are not discarded they are merely part of your adulthood role. It is ironic that under normal developmental conditions, you are supposed to outgrow childhood behaviors when you become an adult. In fact, being an adult means that you no longer are a child.

Yet much of the resistance to change that comes from others is that they want to know or control you as you once were. Allowing this to help will impede the healthy development for the recovering adult child. Part of recovering is learning how to handle resistance. Managing resistance effectively will allow you to go on with your recovery.

Adaptive behavior patterns and childhood roles play a great part in the lives of the adult child. In contrast to childhood, however, the adult child can now begin to assess these behaviors for their positive and negative consequences, retain what is beneficial, and abandon what impedes growth. For the adult child who is attempting to make peace with himself or herself, it is important to remember not to get caught up in the process of role abandonment just for the sake of it. If you truly like who you are and you are functioning well, why change?

A great part of this discussion has been to identify positive and negative characterisitics in adult children and to point out that many parts of adult children are and can be healthy. You can feel good about yourself and still be concerned about issues in your life. Thus the adult child can begin making peace with himself or herself internally, by understanding or changing their adaptive behaviors, and then identifying and working through their major concerns about being an adult child. Knowing, understanding and accepting yourself better will make the process of working through your major concerns easier.

Identifying Major Areas of Concerns for Adult Children

What concerns you the most about being an adult child? How do you know which issues or problems bother you the most? Which would you like to work on first? Answer the questions in Table 4.1 to help you identify your major areas of concerns today (see Table 4.1). In the first part of the table you were able to assess your degree of concern on each item. The second part then asks you to rank these according to how important each area is to you now.

By using this table, you should be able to identify what concerns you the most and which issues you may want to work through first. Not all adult children will share the same degrees of concern, nor will all adult children rank the concerns in the same order or importance. However, these seven areas of concerns were identified as the most important to adult children in the National Adult Children of Alcoholics Research Study. Each of these areas of concerns is related to being an adult child of an alcoholic. However, they are not all directly related to alcoholism or the alcoholic. In fact, only one of the concerns identified mentioned getting the alcoholic sober.

The majority of the concerns were directly related to the adult child. The second interesting observation is that some of the concerns are similar to ones with which any adult may identify.

For example, adult children are not the only adults concerned about their relationships, rearing their children or improving relationships with their parents. Even though these similarities exist, their uniqueness for adult children must be appreciated. Each of these areas can mean something different and more to adult children. In Table 4.2 you will find the results of how the adult children in the national study ranked each of the areas of concern and the degree of concern that was given to each. The table is presented with the areas of concern ranked from the highest to the lowest.

Table 4.1

Areas of Concern for Adult Children of Alcoholics

Degree of Concern

Please indicate your degree of concern in the following areas using this scale:

5 = **Highly concerned**
4 = **Often concerned**
3 = **Moderately concerned**
2 = **Seldom concerned**
1 = **Never concerned**

1. I am concerned about my own alcohol or drug use. _____
2. I am concerned about how to get my parent(s) sober. _____
3. I am concerned about improving the relationship between my parents and me. _____
4. I am concerned about improving my own relationships. _____
5. I am concerned about my spouse's use of alcohol or drugs. _____
6. I am concerned about how to help my children not to be affected by being an adult child of an alcoholic. _____
7. I am concerned about other issues that I feel are related to parental alcoholism. _____

Prioritizing Concerns

Rank the following from highest to lowest according to the degree of importance to you. (1 = highest, 7 = lowest)

1. I am concerned about my own alcohol or drug use. _____
2. I am concerned about how to get my parent(s) sober. _____
3. I am concerned about improving the relationship between my parents and me. _____
4. I am concerned about improving my own relationships. _____
5. I am concerned about my spouse's use of alcohol or drugs. _____
6. I am concerned about how to help my children not to be affected by being an adult child of an alcoholic. _____
7. I am concerned about other issues that I feel are related to parental alcoholism. _____

As indicated on Table 4.2 there were differences in the degree of concern over each item among all adult children. Adult sons and daughters differed not only of the degrees of concern for each item, but also on their ranking of each item. The following is a discussion of the ranking of each concern and how they are especially unique for adult children.

Table 4.2

Areas of Concern for Adult Children of Alcoholics by Degree

Degree of Concern

Please indicate your degree of concern in the following areas using this scale:

5 = **Highly concerned**
4 = **Often concerned**
3 = **Moderately concerned**
2 = **Seldom concerned**
1 = **Never concerned**

I am concerned about . . .	(R)	ACoAs	(R)	Sons	(R)	Daughters
Improving my own relationships	1	4.19	1	4.19	1	4.18
Other issues	2	3.68	2	3.69	2	3.66
How to help my children not to be affected by my being an adult child	3	3.57	3	3.38	2	3.73
Improving the relationship between my parents and between my parents and myself	4	2.75	5	2.63	4	2.84
My own alcohol or drug use	5	2.69	4	2.94	5	2.50
How to get my parent(s) sober	6	1.89	6	1.85	7	1.92
My spouse's use of alcohol or drugs	7	1.85	7	1.42	6	2.22
TOTALS		20.62		20.10		21.05

(R) = Ranking

1. **I am concerned about improving my own relationships.**

   This is the only issue that was ranked the same in Table 4.2 by sons **and** daughters. Of all the issues confronting children of alcoholics in their adult lives, their ability to establish and maintain healthy relationships will be the most critical. If adult children are to improve their lives, many will need to improve their abilities in relationships.

   This issue may have been ranked number one because it is the one area in which adult children characteristics are most likely to surface, but also it is the area in which adult children most want to grow. Many adult children may have entered adulthood with the idea that their relationships would be different, that their families would be close and that their marriages would be trouble-free, only to find that although they had the desire for healthy relationships, they lacked the abilities to achieve them.

   Another factor is that many adult children are extremely competent in many areas, but need improvement in their relationships. In fact, some may feel that they handle everything but relationships. Therefore, the high degree for this concern for adult children is a combination of normal adult development and having been reared in a dysfunctional family with few healthy role models. Thus working through this issue may not only be the most important for establishing healthy relationships, but also it can be the key to working through all of the other issues.

2. **I am concerned about other issues that I feel are related to parental alcoholism.**

   This concern is a collection of all of the other issues that were identified by adult children but not found in the six areas. Tabulated collectively, they ranked second. Between sons and daughters there was a difference in rank of one position, with sons ranking it second and daughters ranking it third. The concerns of this issue range from lack of self-confidence, low self-esteem, job performance problems to overcoming denial and other problems that may have existed in their families. The diversity of concerns was extensive, but the concern identified most came from those adult children who were additionally victimized by being raised in sexually abusive or violent homes.

Although not totally understood, there appears to be an unfortunate correlation between alcohol abuse and domestic violence or sexual abuse in the family. Thus many adult children of alcoholics are in another form of "double jeopardy". Not only are they adult children of alcoholics, but also adults who were victimized as children. Many of these same adult children have witnessed spouse abuse in their families as well.

There are many statistical arguments over the exact nature and relationship between alcohol abuse and child abuse. Some authorities state that the two behaviors occur in a family only about 10% of the time, whereas others argue that as high as 90% of child abuse cases involve excessive drinking.

In the National Adult Children of Alcoholics Research Study the percentages of adult children who were physically or sexually abused or who witnessed spouse abuse fall in between these statistics. The reporting of spouse abuse statistics is included because it is a form of child abuse. That is, if you harm someone or something the child loves, you harm the child. Certainly, witnessing or knowing that your parent is being abused is emotionally abusive for children. Like alcoholism, domestic violence affects the entire family. In Table 4.3 the percentages of adult children of alcoholics who were physically or sexually abused or who lived in a spouse abuse situation are compared with adults of non-alcoholic parents (see Table 4.3). As indicated in Table 4.3, all three forms of abuse were higher for adult children of alcoholics. In the alcoholic home spouse abuse was the highest and in the non-alcoholic family, physical child abuse was the highest. When asked if no abuse occurred at all, including emotional abuse and neglect, only 16.2% of adult children's families indicated that they lived in an abuse-free environment compared to 62.6% of adults of non-alcoholic families.

Table 4.3

**Adult Children of Alcoholics Compared to Adults
of Non-Alcoholic Parents Who Were Abused**

Type of Abuse	ACoA	Non-ACoA
Physical Abuse	28.1%	7.4%
Sexual Abuse	13.8	4.5
Spouse Abuse	35.3	4.1
No Abuse*	16.2	62.6

* (no physical, sexual, emotional, spouse or neglect reported)

Although some adult children disproportionately reported different forms of physical abuse, it is obvious that a high degree of emotional abuse and neglect occurred for many adult children of alcoholics. It is not uncommon, therefore, for adult children to need to address these other issues in treatment. In some cases these issues can be so profound, as in the case of sexual abuse, that the adult child will need to or prefer to work on these issues first.

Making peace with yourself for the adult child will require making peace with all childhood experiences. Often when the adult child confronts the parental alcoholism these other issues will surface. They should not be ignored because the adult child is working on "ACoA" issues, but rather should be expressed and considered as an indicator of growth. As one is growing vertically, the new growth may give strength to working on other silent issues.

3. **I am concerned about how to help my children not to be affected by my being an adult child of an alcoholic.**

On Table 4.2 women ranked this concern one position higher than men. This issue focuses not only on the desire of many adult children to be healthy parents, but also for their children to be reared differently than they were. This issue is related to guessing at what is normal.

Since many adult children did not have the "ideal" parental role models as children, it leaves them without these models to be parents. Many of the attitudes about parenting are learned as a child. The adult child may feel that he or she is parenting without a set of adequate guidelines. On top of all this may be the desire to be a "perfect" parent. By now you hope to have worked through your perfectionist tendencies better than anyone else, of course.

What do parenting issues, however, have to do with adult children issues? Quite simply, parenting will put an adult in touch with his or her own childhood. Your children often remind you of yourself at that age and of the accompanying parental behavior. Therefore, parenting yourself will put you in contact with the parenting you received. The adult child who becomes a parent and has a genuine concern for his or her abilities to be a healthy parent is a growing adult child. The adult child is now achieving what Erikson calls generativity or the ability to give beyond oneself to the next generation (Erikson, 1963). Consider and accept your concern as an indicator of your growth.

4. I am concerned about improving the relationship between my parents and between my parents and me.

This issue is divided into two levels of concern about parental relationships. On the one level the adult child is concerned about improving the relationship between his or her parents. That is, the adult child would like Mother and Father to get along better. This appears to be a very legitimate concern since we know from earlier research that children of alcoholics are far more upset about the parental relationship than they are the drinking (Cork, 1969).

The second level involves improving the relationship between you and your parents, i.e., you would like to get along better with one or both of your parents. Often an indicator of growth is wanting to share your experience. Many adult children want to share it with their parents, either to improve existing relationships or to establish ones that never existed. For many adult children, making peace with themselves will include attempting to do things they have always wanted to try. Improving parental relationships may be one.

5. **I am concerned about my own alcohol or drug use.**

It is commonly agreed that children of alcoholics are much more likely than children of non-alcoholics to develop alcoholism, so this concern is justified. Findings indicate that not only are children of alcoholics at a greater risk to develop alcoholism, but also that many will begin drinking at an early age. Additionally, many recovering alcoholics are adult children of alcoholics and vice versa. As indicated on Table 4.2, sons of alcoholics have a higher score on this issue and rank it higher than daughters. This may be caused by several factors, such as sons of alcoholics developing alcohol problems more than do daughters or by the fact that there appears to be a higher rate of addiction among males in general in our population.

Often it is their own addiction that brings many adult children into contact with their own issues about being the child of an alcoholic. Addicted adult children are in double jeopardy. It is important to remember that although two problems exist, the active addiction must be handled first. Adult children issues may contribute to the addiction, but they cannot be used as an excuse or rationalization to avoid addressing the active addiction. Additionally, adult children issues can be addressed in recovery, but only as an adjunct to becoming chemical-free. Attempting to resolve adult children issues while chemically dependent is similar to counseling a person who is intoxicated. The chemical dependency must stop first.

Another related issue is at what point should the recovering chemically dependent person begin to work on adult children issues? Although there is no set guideline for this question, it is commonly felt that at least one year of chemical sobriety is necessary. Likewise, it is important to consider the impact of working on adult children issues on the maintaining of sobriety. For example, if raising adult children issues increases the probability of relapse for the recovering person, then the adult children issues will have to wait. Addressing some adult children issues too early in recovery may cause an "emotional relapse", which can lead to returning to substance abuse.

6. I am concerned about how to get my parent(s) sober.

Sons and daughters ranked this concern differently, with sons ranking it one position higher than did daughters. Unfortunately, the majority of alcoholics do not stop drinking, and even though the adult child no longer lives at home, this does not diminish the desire for the parent to get sober. Getting the parent sober is a legitimate concern for the adult child, but it is interesting how many other issues were ranked ahead of it. However, this can be considered as a healthy sign that adult children feel a need to work on their own issues first. Children of alcoholics cannot get sober for their parents. You may want, encourage and facilitate treatment for your parent, but you cannot achieve sobriety for another person. The adult child may have to make peace with this issue. In reality, it is part of making peace with yourself because it requires you to begin to accept those things you cannot change.

This raises another issue for many adult children — responsibility. That is, is it the responsibility of adult children to get the parent sober? No. It is the responsibility of the alcoholic. This does not mean you cannot arrange for an intervention for the alcoholic parent. However, you can do so by choice, rather than from an unnecessary feeling of guilt or responsibility.

Finally, the adult child must accept that the parent may never get sober and must go on with his or her life. This requires building support systems outside of your family to facilitate your own growth. Adult children who feel that the parent must get sober before they can work on their own issues as adult children are continuing to allow themselves to be dominated, not only by the alcoholic but also by the alcoholism.

7. I am concerned about my spouse's use of alcohol or drugs.

This issue was ranked last by sons of alcoholics and next to the last by daughters. The higher ranking given by daughters of alcoholics is probably caused by the fact that more of them find themselves married to a substance-abusing male than do the sons of alcoholics.

This appears to be clinically valid as well, since it is not uncommon for daughters of alcoholics to marry a male who eventually will become alcoholic. It does not appear that sons of alcoholics marry women who become alcoholics as often. Additionally, given the low ranking of this issue in general, it appears that many adult children do not marry spouses who develop substance-abuse problems.

Those adult children whose spouses have developed substance-abuse problems, however, also find themselves in a position of double jeopardy. The adult child in this position now finds herself confronted not only with adult children issues, but also with being the spouse of a substance abuser. The adult child in this situation will be faced with several critical issues.

One issue focuses on whose needs are to be met first, the adult child's or the addicted spouse's. Another is, does the adult child feel he or she has the ability or the resources to handle the addicted spouse situation? Finally, the issue of responsibility for someone else's sobriety surfaces again. Above all of the issues might be the feeling on the part of the adult child of "How could I have let this happen?" or "I should have known better". The adult child may feel that since he or she was reared with alcoholism, this problem should have been avoided in his or her own marriage. Thus the adult child literally may blame himself or herself for the situation.

Very few people ever marry a chemically dependent person. The spouse who becomes addicted usually does so well into a marriage. Adult children are not responsible for causing addiction. The adult child in this situation first must become aware of and act on his or her needs as an adult child before considering facilitating and supporting someone else's recovery. Adult children must not let someone else's addiction or recovery become a prerequisite to their own growth. Additionally, the adult child spouse who is recovering will be in a better position emotionally and psychologically to handle spouse addiction.

Unresolved or unhealthy issues in the adult child will impede the understanding of and intervention in the addicted spouse's unhealthy behaviors. Someone's issues in this situation need to be handled first, and if you are the adult child, then yours come first. You can handle your own recovery; you can only facilitate another's recovery. You will be a better facilitator if you are at peace with yourself.

These seven areas of concerns are some of the issues that most concern adult children of alcoholics, but each adult child will have his or her own degree and ranking regarding each concern. Additionally, other considerations may be involved in recovery for the adult child. Making peace for the adult child will require working through all of his or her concerns today about being an adult child. Unresolved issues will lead only to a "fragile peace" that will be emotionally shattered each time the concern is confronted without satisfactory resolution.

Resolution does not mean that the situation is corrected or resolved, but rather that it is now emotionally manageable. Part of making peace is the understanding that you no longer must "fix" everything in order for it to be all right. You can learn to be and feel all right about yourself. How you feel about yourself and your concerns will be more important than the resolution of each concern.

Making Peace With Your Feelings

So far this chapter has addressed making peace with yourself by understanding and looking at yourself, assessing your adaptive behavior patterns, abandoning childhood behaviors and roles and identifying your major areas of concerns as an adult child. Critical to achieving all of these will be your ability to make peace with your feelings today about being an adult child. Unresolved issues contain unresolved feelings. What and which feelings are the strongest in you today?

Although each adult child has individual feelings about being an adult child, there are many feelings which are common among all adult children. These include, but are not limited to, feeling angry, resentful, betrayed, abandoned, fearful, rejected, inferior, cheated, guilty or manipulated. All of these feelings not only are negative, but maintaining them will impede the adult child in making peace with himself or herself. Adult children can possess some positive feelings as well, which include feeling competent, being a survivor, mature, successful, reliable, independent, hopeful and content.

The adult child will need to work through negative feelings to release energy to develop and grow in healthy directions. Maintaining resentments, for example, will require energy for negative use which could be used elsewhere positively.

Making peace with your feelings is a process, not a cure. Of all the processes in this chapter, however, it may be the most difficult. You may be able to rationalize your way through all of the other processes and still feel empty, because you have not felt your way through your feelings. There are no specific treatment strategies designed just for feelings. Each adult child will need to experiment and invest energy into how best to work through his or her feelings. This may involve individual counseling, group work, sharing your feelings with other adult children, working through issues with significant others or making a realistic evaluation of yourself. Each adult child may find he or she will want to follow some of the following suggestions.

1. **Do not punish yourself over your childhood.**

   You did not create it. You did not cause it. You can overcome it. Holding yourself accountable for conditions you could not control will inhibit your growth. You now can learn to control your feelings about the past, and you can learn to control how you feel today.

2. **Treat yourself with respect.**

   Remember, you are not a second-class citizen. You no longer need to subjugate your feelings because of fear, guilt or embarrassment. Once you have worked through these feelings, you should be able to elevate yourself to a position of self-respect. If *you* do not respect your feelings, how can anyone else? As a child or an adult, you may have thought that somebody would come along and do something about your condition. Well, you are a *somebody*.

3. **Let go of your negative feelings.**

   Do not allow yourself to be robbed of the energy necessary to improve your life. Keeping old feelings

does not leave room for new ones. It is similar to
asking, "Why do I always feel this way?" The answer is
— because you always feel this way. Try other feelings
by first letting go of the negative ones. You must learn
to let them go. It takes energy to be angry, and, it takes
energy to grow. The energy must come from somewhere, so make room for growth within yourself by
freeing up the energy you already possess.

4. **Recognize that feeling and doing are two different
things.**

In order to change, you must change. Recovery,
contrary to popular belief, does not occur by osmosis.
In order to truly change, you must live the change.
Without action the desire to change remains only a
desire. You have been hoping long enough. Now try
doing.

5. **Make peace with all of the parts of yourself.**

Now that you are aware of the many different areas
or concerns you may have as an adult child, you will
need to make peace with all of you. Do not be afraid to
acknowledge all of your feelings. You have been
feeling them, why not acknowledge them? Awareness
and acknowledgment can be the first steps to change.
Making peace with all parts of you should not be
confused with making peace with everyone or everything that ever happened to you. It means making
peace with all of your feelings about these things. To
make peace with only half of yourself may mean that
you will remain in a constant struggle between the two
sides. The unresolved side will always attempt to
control you and impede your growth. Even though you
may have been out of balance as a child do not remain
out of balance as an adult.

6. **Affirm yourself.**

Do not be afraid to assert your positive behaviors or
feelings. Do not be afraid to acknowledge your assets
and capabilities. You are a survivor. You have made it
this far. You have the abilities to grow. You are a
somebody. You can affirm that "I am an adult child
and I am becoming . . ."

As stated above, making peace with yourself is a process. How long it takes and how far you will grow depends upon your capacity and desire for growth. Not all adult children will be able to achieve the same degree of inner peace. Whatever degree you can achieve is worth the effort. It is much better than allowing your past to dictate your future. The adult child who is at peace will be able to go beyond his or her childhood experiences and identity. Inner peace will allow the adult child to better handle external events. Additionally, many adult children will want to translate their new inner peace into making amends with others who have influenced their lives.

Adult children must be able to make peace with themselves, before they attempt to make peace with others. The adult child should remember that if he or she is at peace, then making amends with others will always be an addition to one's life, not a substitute.

Once inner peace is achieved, it is yours to maintain. No one can take it from you any more than they could create it for you.

5

Making Peace
With Your Family

The most powerful influence on young children of alcoholics is the family. This influence, as in all families, has both positive and negative consequences for children, not only in their childhood but in adulthood as well. In healthy families there are more positive consequences, but for many adult children, the negative consequences outnumber the positive ones and tend to be maintained in adulthood.

Children have no choice over family impact, but adults do have a choice. As adult children, this impact can remain unchanged, increase or decrease. Adult children can influence the amount and type of family association, and perhaps more importantly they can learn to control their feelings, positive and negative, about their families.

Although adult children of alcoholics may feel as adults now they are away from their families and are no longer concerned, this is not the case. As was noted in the previous chapter: four of the seven major areas of concerns for adult children of alcoholics had to do with family issues.

Family concerns for adult children manifest themselves in four areas which can be found both in the adult's family of orientation, the one in which they were reared, and in their family of procreation, if and when they rear their own families. Within these two families lie the four concerns.

In the family of orientation the adult child may want to make peace with his or her parents or siblings. In the family of procreation the adult child may be concerned about having a harmonious relationship with his or her spouse and children. For adult children of alcoholics, making peace with the family is a major concern.

Making peace with your family should be attempted only after making peace with yourself. If achieved, it should add to your growth and not be used as a substitute or excuse for not recovering yourself. You first must make peace with yourself. This will allow you the assurance of knowing your inner harmony is not dependent upon someone else's. If it is, then you are co-dependent and not really at peace. If you must wait for your family to recover first, does this mean you cannot recover until after they recover? What happens if they do not recover? If all family members in alcoholic families are not affected the same, not all recovering at the same rate or degree, then why wait for a singular occurrence that may not happen?

Family recovery is a goal. It is not a prerequisite to your own recovery. First, you must recover. Share your recovery if you wish, but be strong enough in your own recovery if your family rejects recovery for themselves. Your goal cannot be to change your family because only they can change themselves. Your goal is to make a kind of peace with them that will work for you.

Do not let your ideas and ideals about family life interfere with your common sense. Accept both yourself and your family for what all of you really are, not what you fantasize all of you should be. You can learn to make peace only if it is based on reality. Fantasy maintains denial and disproportionately raises expectations that will never be achieved.

For many adult children, making peace with their families will not only be their second most difficult task, but also the first one they want to achieve after making peace with themselves. But remember, making peace with yourself comes *first*. There are many reasons for this.

1. Family is the most significant emotional influence on adult children, as is the case for most people.

2. Many adult children want the close family they never actually had and will try to make their family closer. Their goal in attempting to make peace with their family is to try to become the close family they have always pretended to be. It is ironic that many adult children maintain the "myth of family closeness" and at the same time want the family to change. If the family was so close, why the desire to change? In many instances, the only way in which the family was close was in sharing and maintaining the "family secret".

3. Recovery can be contagious. Often an indicator of growth is wanting to share it. One of the first places many adult children want to share their growth is with their families.

4. Wanting to love and be loved by our families is a strong need. Emotional neglect, the inability to meet one's needs emotionally, occurs in many alcoholic families. Adult children, therefore, may try to give to their families what they hope to get in return.

5. Relationships that end on a bad note never end. Even though the adult child has moved away from the family, he or she does not leave the emotional impact behind. The adult child may feel a strong need to find a resting place for the emotional "ties that bind".

6. You may have a desire to achieve external peace with people in your life. Once inner peace is achieved, the adult child may desire an outer peace in his or her life, particularly with family members.

7. You may want to make your family of procreation different from the one in which you were raised. This goal means that you do not want any unfinished business from your childhood or relationships with your parents or siblings to affect your relationships with your spouse or children.

Regardless of your motivations for wanting to make peace with your family, it will be a challenging experience. Not all adult children will want to undertake this endeavor. Each adult child must determine the need to achieve family harmony, the amount of energy to be invested, what are realistic expectations and his or her own motivations.

It is important to remember that it is not your responsibility to become the *family counselor*. Although it is admirable to want to share your recovery, this does not make you a family therapist. You are a member of the family, not its therapist.

Keep in mind that there is a fine line between being supportive and being used. Your goal is not to change your family members; you are not responsible for their growth. Making peace with your family is for your own benefit. If other family members indirectly grow from your efforts or seek recovery themselves, that is an added benefit, not the original goal.

Prior to making peace with your family, you will need to determine what issues need to be confronted. Additionally, you will need to determine which family members you will need to work with the most. You cannot expect to work through the issues involving one family member only by discussing it with everyone but that person.

However, when it comes to families we all have at least two: the family that we experience and the one we carry inside ourselves. Making peace with the family or family member inside you is the most important one. An adult child who is able to make peace with his or her inner parent may state, "I am content with how I understand and view my parents today." This may or may not mean that the adult child would like to get along better with the parent; it means that the adult child has accepted himself or herself and the relationship between the parents for what it is. It means that you now have the ability to be in harmony with yourself, knowing that you have made an honest effort to make peace with your inner parent.

Finally, you must realize that all issues in alcoholic families cannot be blamed on alcoholism. Even normal families have problems. The adult child must be able to separate what are alcohol-related problems from normal family problems. This is not to say that alcoholism does not compound normal family problems, only that a certain number of issues are present in all families. Nor should you expect all problems to disappear after making peace with your family. However, you should be able to handle them more realistically.

Although there are four areas in which the adult child may want to make peace with his or her family, living in harmony with their parents is probably paramount for adult children. Of the four areas, the parental relationship may have had the longest impact, the greatest emotional impact and can continue to affect the adult child negatively.

Making Peace With Your Parents

Making peace with your parent(s) is a two-part process. One is to make peace with your inner parent — the parent you carry around inside of you. It contains the imprints, messages, values, conflicts and feelings that have been internalized by you because of your contact with your parents.

The other parents are the actual persons. You will need first to make peace with your inner parent and if you then cannot achieve peace with the actual parent, at least the one that accompanies you every day will be acceptable.

Making peace with parents is a complex process and will raise many issues for the adult child. Throughout the entire process, the adult child will be faced with choices. The most critical of these will be either to maintain existing opinions, injuries and negative implications or to let them go. You can choose to keep old patterns alive or you can seek alternatives. Each adult child will need to determine what are the inner and actual relationships with his or her parent.

Not all adult children will feel a strong need to make peace with parents. Some adult children will not want to, others will not know how. Some adult children will have parents who continue to behave in ways that make fence-mending impossible.

Do You Need to Make Peace With Your Parents?

How do you know if you need to make peace with your parents? Do you need to make peace with both of them or only one? What is the conflict over which you need to make peace? All of these questions need to be answered by the adult child in order to establish a better understanding of your desire to make peace with your parents. Additionally, what do you expect from making peace? How will this contribute to your own growth?

To answer these questions, make a list of all the things you would like to say to your parent. Since we are starting with the inner parent, keep the list to yourself. We are attempting individual growth, not running the United Nations. Make a list of what bothers you most about your parents. Make a list of the things you would like to change about how you feel about your parents. In order to balance some of your perspectives and feelings, also make a list of the things you would like to keep with your parents. What are the things that they have taught you that serve you well today? Once you have completed your lists, you will have a clearer understanding of the issues and feelings which really concern you.

Additionally, do you want to make peace only with the inner parents, or are you going to try it with the real parents as well? Since you are working at two different levels, be prepared to have two different responses.

For example, you may be able to achieve a healthy relationship with your inner parents, but not the same level with the real parents. The opposite also may be true: You can achieve a "workable" relationship with your real parents, but not with your inner parents. You may work through issues with one of your parents better than with the other, so do not expect miracles; settle for a workable peace.

Your Inner Parents

Your inner parents are the ones who are emotionally inside of you. They are the parts of your parents that have become a part of you. Your inner parents affect you positively and negatively. Some adult children will have totally different perceptions of their parents than others. Some adult children feel that, although there was parental alcoholism, their parents did the best they could do. Other adult children feel extremely deprived. The majority will fall somewhere in between.

Working to achieve peace with the inner parents will be to stop blaming your parents for how you feel today. Yes, they were or perhaps still are a great part of your life, but you now have a choice and the ability to control your emotional responses to things you do not like. You may not be able to change people and circumstances, but you can learn to change your emotional responses. Thus most of making peace with the inner parent is achieved by letting go of negative responses that continue to affect you in a harmful way.

Approach your task by making one major assumption — that your parents will not change. This is the safest position because you are working with the inner parent first, and if you work with the real parents later, you will not raise unrealistic expectations of change.

This view is shared by Harold Bloomfield in his book *Making Peace with Your Parents*. Bloomfield says that the adult must change his or her own emotional response, not the parents' response by doing the following (Bloomfield, 1985).

1. Diffuse guilt.

One of the major feelings often expressed by adult children of alcoholics is guilt. The source of this guilt can vary. It may come from feeling responsible for causing the alcoholism or for not being able to stop it. The adult child may believe that he or she avoided the problem or denied it. Some adult children may feel they themselves were the problem in the family. Others may feel that it was their fault that their parents did not get along better.

Whatever the source of the guilt, one thing is common. Children of alcoholics do not cause any of the above behaviors in their parents. Most of the guilt felt by adult children is extremely perplexing, because they feel guilty but are not sure why. If you do not own the source, let it go. Whoever or whatever makes you feel guilty, controls you. If your inner parents make you feel guilty, realistically assess your part in causing the behavior over which you feel guilty and respond accordingly. Most of the time this response will diffuse unnecessary guilt. You will come to realize that you were not the cause of the things about which you have felt guilty.

Adult children may have guilt over childhood events and over adult behaviors. This may be particularly true about how the adult child handles family relationships today. They may not want to visit their family because of the alcoholism, yet feel guilty for not visiting. They may want to confront the alcoholic, but they continue to support denial systems. In this manner the internal guilt influences external behavior and maintains a cycle that must be broken.

Guilt is not the only feeling that adult children may need to diffuse. Other feelings might include resentment, betrayal, denial, responsibility or abandonment. Whatever the feelings, their impact on the adult child will be lessened and inner peace will be increased if they can be eliminated, controlled or diffused.

2. Retrain emotional habits.

Do you emotionally respond the same way every time your parent does the same thing? If peace is to be achieved at least one of you must change. There is a higher probability that it can be you. Your emotional responses are not limited only to behaviors either. A particular parental imprint may generate the same emotional response every time you remember it. No one is going to remove it from your memory, but you can change how you respond to it emotionally.

The adult child can work through his or her memories, and eventually the intensity that once accompanied remembering begins to change. The goal is not to avoid remembering, but to be able to control your response to the memory.

For example, your parents always pull your same strings when you visit, or they are always singing the same negative emotional song. How do you respond? Do you sing and dance? After all, you know the music and the steps by heart, or do you realize that now you have a choice? Do you know why your parents can "push your buttons"? It is because they installed them! Again, you cannot change their habits. That is not your responsibility, but you can change your own emotional habits.

3. Understand your parents' childhood.

Just as you are influenced by your childhood, so were your parents influenced by theirs. As an adult child, you may feel that many of your behaviors and characteristics are caused by having been reared in an alcoholic family. In what kind of families were your parents reared? Was one (or both) of your parents reared in an alcoholic family? Understanding your parents' childhood may help you to understand not only their behaviors better, but also their motivations. You may have been more upset with why they did or said certain things than that they did them.

There is a big difference between understanding, approval and acceptance. You do not need to approve of behavior, but you can learn to understand the motivations for it. If you can understand why, you may find acceptance easier. If you want to be understood for who you are, understand them for who they are.

Often your parents' childhood is the key to understanding them better. If you decide to try this, spend time with your parents. Ask questions about your grandparents and how your parents were reared. What influenced your parents as children? What childhood memories are the most important, most painful or happiest? Talk with relatives and friends who knew your parents as they were growing up. Explore what insights they can offer you. You are trying to make peace, and awareness of what you are working with will contribute to the process. Do not be afraid to understand and to accept their childhood in order to accept yours.

4. Break free of the approval trap.

This statement is a good example of something "easier said than done". It means that the adult child must stop engaging in behaviors only to seek parental approval. If these behaviors were healthy ones, this would be no problem. Given the parameters of most alcoholic families and childrens' needs not to be abandoned, however, there is a strong likelihood that many behaviors were performed to meet dysfunctional family guidelines. In order to break free of any negative family norms, the adult child must stop engaging in behaviors that fit these rules.

The desire to be accepted and belong is strong in all families, but gaining acceptance under dysfunctional conditions will inhibit the growth of the individual family member. The adult child who is stuck in the approval trap is controlled externally. Breaking free of this emotional habit requires growth and strength.

Judging what is best for you requires healthy guidelines. If your external approval trap is based on unhealthy ones, you will need to change them. You will need to develop your own set of guidelines, however. If you keep any of your parents guidelines, do it by choice, not because you are in a trap.

5. Visit without unrealistic expectations.

Do not set yourself up for disappointments by raising your expectations for new behavior from your parents when you visit. You are the one who is growing; they may remain unchanged. Bring your expectations down to a realistic level. If your parents go beyond them, you can be pleasantly surprised. If they do not, you are prepared. This does not mean, however, always to expect the worst. Always expecting the worst only leads to a self-fulfilling prophecy or to thinking that things will never change.

Do not fall into an all or nothing pattern, but instead balance your expectations. You must be particularly cautious not to expect too much too fast when things start to improve. Change is a process which requires time and practice. Relapses will occur, and these, too, should be a part of your expectations.

If sobriety occurs for the alcoholic parent, do not expect everything to be normal. What is normal may be an entirely new behavior for all members of the family. New behaviors and communication patterns will need to be developed in order for family growth to occur. Do not raise your expectations too high, because very little may change after sobriety. Family members may stay on a "dry drunk" syndrome without going any further in recovery. Sobriety alone guarantees nothing; it only potentiates it. Actual recovery requires both energy and change.

6. Develop your own support family.

If your family will not support you, find those who will. The absence of family support does not mean that all support is unavailable. You do not have to be alone unless you choose to be. You have a choice. Use it.

Alternative support systems can be found among your friends, other relatives or fellow adult children of alcoholics. Seek out these systems or if they come to you, do not be afraid to accept their help. You do not need to recover alone. There are people other than your parents to help you make peace with your parents, especially with your inner parent.

Additionally, adult children of alcoholics are not the only adults who are trying to make peace with their parents. It is a common concern, endured by most and shared by few. Many adults may be looking for support with these issues. You are not alone. Reading this book is a form of a support system; you are supporting yourself with additional insight and knowledge.

Adult children who are parents can work on developing a healthy family and communication skills with your spouse and children. If you want a healthy family environment, try developing it in your own family.

7. The goal is not to change your parents.

If you try to change your parents, you will lose sight of your original goal, making peace with your inner parents. There are two reasons not to try to change your parents before making peace with your inner parents: (1) Your peace is conditional upon changing your parents, (2) If they do not change, you are stuck. The goals are for you. You must be able to achieve the goals alone, without asking or relying on anyone else to do it for you.

In addition, trying to change your parents may consume too much of your energy and leave little for self-growth. If you have made peace with yourself, you can accept your parents for who they are. Who they are will not destroy what you have accomplished.

Obviously, unchanged and difficult parents can continue to have an impact on you, but, keeping your goals properly focused will help to reduce the impact. If your parents refuse to change and you keep trying to change them, the only one who ends up being different is you. Be yourself; you will be easier to live with.

8. During changes you may need to maintain a "safe" distance.

If thinking about your parents causes you an emotional relapse or if visiting them makes you feel insecure or small, put some psychological and physical distance between you. The handling of difficult times often requires alternative behaviors. You may need to have more time to yourself to work through your issues.

If you visit your parents too soon, too often, or stay too long you may feel that you are being pulled back into old patterns that inhibit your growth. Part of growth is knowing your limits, knowing when you are vulnerable, so do not try to handle too much too soon. Listen to yourself and allow your feelings to come forth.

For example, you may need to structure your visits with your parents to reduce problems. If you normally visit for a day and everything is fine for a few hours and then deteriorates, plan to leave after only a few hours. Change your patterns of interactions with your parents to find alternatives.

Learn not to put yourself into positions that you cannot handle well. There is a difference between avoiding an issue and knowing when departure is a healthy alternative.

9. Your life first, theirs second.

This does not mean that you are callous and do not care about your parents. It does mean that you can take a legitimate interest in yourself and feel comfortable doing it. It means your growth first, theirs second, and that neither is co-dependent upon the other. If growth occurs in both, then a healthy sense of inter-dependency can develop.

10. Be at peace with all of the times that you have had.

Adult children should not be ashamed of who they are, where they have been, or their past. All of these things have contributed to who you are today. Some of these contributions have been positive while others have been negative and painful. Do not be afraid to work on any issue with your inner parent. You have survived it; you can survive making peace with it. Not all issues will be dealt with at the same time, nor will all issues require the same amount of emotional investment, but all issues should be dealt with. Make peace with each of them, because they all are a part of you. Do not settle for less than a total and lasting inner peace. You deserve nothing less.

Understanding Your Parents

Understanding your parents includes understanding how and why they parented you the way they did. As mentioned earlier you can learn more about your parents' childhoods in order to better undertand them as people. How they parented you may include additional factors, however, these could include their motivations for having children, their attitudes about parenting, their value systems, or parenting skills.

The most powerful factor influencing parenting skills, however, may have been their marital relationship. The best thing parents can give children is the subject of much debate. Is it love, support, an education, money, guidance or is it that the parents get along with each other?

The spouse relationship affects the parenting relationship. Research indicates that children (in alcoholic families) are more upset by the relationship between their parents than they are by the drinking of the alcoholic (Cork, 1969). A troubled marital relationship often will produce trouble for children, thus adult children may be better able to understand their parents by understanding the spouse relationship. Parenting while under spousal stress affects the parental performance. There are two ways to begin to understand how the two are interrelated.

One way is to understand the relationship between your parents' marriage and how it affected their parenting skills, positively or negatively. Another way is to examine the effects of their relationship on you. Unfortunately, ideal marital relationships are not the norm in alcoholic families.

Table 5.1 reflects how adult children of alcoholics and adults from non-alcoholic parents rate the relationship between their parents while they were growing up.

Table 5.1

Adult Children of Alcoholic and Non-Alcoholic Parents Perceptions of the Quality of Their Parents' Relationship

Quality of Parents' Relationship	Non-ACoA	ACoA
Above average	44.6%	11.0%
Average	28.7	24.8
Below Average	26.7	64.2

As indicated in the above table, there appears to be a great difference in the quality of marital relationships in alcoholic families compared to non-alcoholic families. Marital relationships in alcoholic families disproportionately were perceived by adult children as below average. In non-alcoholic families the marital relationship was most commonly perceived as above average. Approximately two-thirds of adult children were reared in families where their parents were fulfilling the parental role while the spouse role was under stress. Therefore, many adult children of alcoholics not only were exposed to alcoholism as children, but also to parents who were under relationship stress. The adult child who was reared with this combination may perceive his or her parents differently than the one-third of adult children who rated their parents' relationship as average or above average.

Understanding how your parents reared you includes understanding the emotional conditions that affected their role performance. Unfortunately, in the stressful marriage, much of the parents' energy may have been consumed in the adult relationships, leaving little for the children. Adult children may wonder why one or both of the parents did not contribute more, love more, understand better or have a more positive attitude about the family. Although you can not change the loss of these, it is easier to make peace with the loss if you can understand the motivation. The alcoholic parent or the non-alcoholic parent may have done the best that he or she could do, given the circumstances. This obviously does not mean that it was the best way to rear children or that what occurred was condoned. Few parents actively or intentionally try to damage their children emotionally.

The Alcoholic Parent

Making peace with an alcoholic parent will be influenced by whether or not the alcoholic parent is recovering. Making peace with someone who is chemically dependent is extremely difficult. In this situation, making peace with the inner parent becomes even more imperative. Unfortunately, as indicated in Table 5.2, the majority of alcoholic parents do not seek treatment, much less achieve sobriety.

Table 5.2

Percentage of Alcoholic Parents Who Sought Treatment	
Did seek treatment	20.1%
Did not seek treatment	79.9%

Therefore, the majority of adult children must attempt to achieve peace with a parent who is still drinking. The adult child must remember that the goal is not to change the parent. This is important when considering active alcoholic parents. It is not the responsibility of adult children to get their alcoholic parents sober. You can facilitate the process if you choose, but it is not your obligation. Your parent's sobriety is not a condition of your own recovery.

You do not have to confront your alcoholic parent, but you can confront the feelings that you carry around inside of you. This does not mean that you do not want to get the parent into treatment. Many adult children will feel an overwhelming need to achieve this. Often the relationship with the alcoholic parent develops feelings within adult children that are difficult to understand. One of these feelings is emotional attachment.

According to research it is not uncommon for children of alcoholics to have a greater emotional attachment for the alcoholic parent than for the non-alcoholic parent (Moos, 1984). Not only is this alarming to many adult children, but also ironic. How could adult children have a greater emotional attachment to the parent who may have caused the greatest emotional strain in their lives?

There can be a variety of explanations for this phenomenon. One explanation, however, is that emotional attachment can mean both positive and negative attachment. The adult child must determine whether his or her motivation for wanting to make peace with the alcoholic parent stems from a positive or negative emotional attachment. Are you trying to get a person who never accepted you to accept you, or are you trying to help someone, or are you attempting both?

If the alcoholic parent and you were never close, you may be trying to get closer. Some adult children want to get farther away from the alcoholic, rather than closer to them. Some will want to get out from under the emotional control exercised by the alcoholic parent. If you feel that you want to confront the alcoholic parent, do so when you both are straight and chemical free. If you feel that you want to confront, but fear a face-to-face visit, write him or her a letter. In your letter be honest with your feelings as you want to express them, not what you want to change in your parent. The goal of your letter is to assist you in making inner peace with yourself, not to make a point with the alcoholic.

Another consideration for the adult child is to be careful that other family members do not expect you to treat or get the alcoholic into treatment. This is especially true for adult children who have sought help for themselves.

Other family members may feel that since you are the one who is dealing with the family alcoholism, you can be the one to handle the alcoholic. Do not support their denial. Family members should not attempt treatment on each other. If other family members are concerned about the parents' active alcoholism, encourage them to seek help for themselves first. When they tell you that they do not have any problems, do not get pulled into the "denial game". It is a waste of your time.

Avoid being pulled into this game with the alcoholic parent also. Whether or not the parent thinks that he or she is alcoholic is not the point. The adult child thinks so. Getting trapped in the denial game can cause the adult child to reconsider if he or she really needs to make peace in the first place. If you have read to this point in this book, you are aware that now is not the time to reinforce denial. People who are not concerned about their weight, do not read diet books. Your perception of the drinking problem is the one that counts. It is this perception and all of the ramifications of having an alcoholic parent that are involved in making peace.

Finally, making peace with the alcoholic parent can be facilitated by making peace with alcoholism. If you do not consider it a disease and regard it as a moral problem, lack of will power or a harmful habit, you will have greater difficulty making peace with your parent.

Alcoholism is a disease. The alcoholic parent is ill. Condemnation and blaming are not part of this disease. Recovery for those surrounded by this disease cannot be found in accusations, causes, guilt or denial.

The Non-Alcoholic Parent

Making peace with your parents is not limited to making peace only with the alcoholic parent. Although it may seem obvious that since the alcoholic parent is the one with the alcoholism, he or she is the major source of all parental issues for the adult child. This is not the case.

If you were reared by two parents, even if only one was alcoholic, you were affected by both of them. Additionally, both of them were affected by alcoholism. This in turn affected their ability to be healthy parents. In many situations the non-alcoholic spouse becomes co-dependent upon the alcoholic spouse. This situation inhibits the functioning of the non-alcoholic and adversely impairs the parenting skills of the non-alcoholic parent.

This impediment can occur in many forms, all of which involve the child. No matter what strategies are used by non-alcoholic parents, they are still parenting under the stress of living with an alcoholic spouse. Some non-alcoholic parents will attempt to deny everything because they feel that the alcoholism is a reflection on them or their marriage. Others feel that denial will protect the children. Adult children may therefore feel uncomfortable with the need to make peace with the non-alcoholic parent, because this parent may have tried harder than the alcoholic to be a successful parent.

Another factor is that not all non-alcoholic parents are alike, and consequently their parental impacts on their adult children will differ. Some non-alcoholic parents can be very successful as compensatory factors for the alcoholic in their children's lives. This was found to be true in the adult children study in Poland in 1974 (Obuchowska, 1974). In this study, among those adult children who were very content in their adult lives, the most common factor was that they all had a very positive image of how their non-alcoholic parent parented them. These non-alcoholic parents were able to be powerfully offsetting factors for their children.

Other studies indicate a need for understanding the adult child and non-alcoholic parent relationship. It was found in some studies that the more time that passed in silence between the adult child and his or her non-alcoholic parent about the family alcoholism, the greater the chances of a negative reaction to the non-alcoholic parent's handling of the situation.

Adult children may have entirely different issues to work through with non-alcoholic parents than with alcoholic parents. The adult child who possesses negative feelings about the non-alcoholic parent relationship often faces such concerns as feeling guilty, wondering why the alcoholism was denied, not being allowed to communicate his or her feelings, being told not to upset the alcoholic, being neglected, feeling unloved or being put into positions that forced them to choose between the two parents.

Whatever the feelings or issues, adult children should not underestimate the need to make peace with non-alcoholic parents. The alcoholism in your family is part of your shared history with this parent. Making peace will require acknowledging and working through this part of your relationship. Some adult children and non-alcoholic parents, like many who go through a crisis together, will feel close. Others will lose their abilities to be close, because surviving the alcoholism has drained them of their emotional energy.

It is important that adult children understand the impact of alcoholism in one spouse on the role fulfillment of the other spouse. All non-alcoholic parents rear their children under the influence of being married to an alcoholic. Given this situation, what is the best they can do? Again, making peace with the inner parents often requires not only understanding them better, but also the conditions under which they functioned and in many cases are still functioning.

Unfortunately, not many non-alcoholic parents seek treatment either. Table 5.3 illustrated that fewer non-alcoholic parents sought treatment than did alcoholics, as shown in Table 5.2.

Table 5.3

Percentage of Non-Alcoholic Parents Who Sought Treatment

Did seek treatment	11.5%	(n= 52)
Did not seek treatment	88.5%	(n=399)

Whatever the reasons for not seeking treatment, many non-alcoholic parents will want to believe that they were not affected. If their adult children raise parenting issues that are related to alcoholism, the non-alcoholic parent may see this not only as a reflection upon themselves, but also as a suggestion that he or she should seek treatment.

Adult children in this situation should be careful not to get caught up in a debate over whether or not the non-alcoholic parent was affected. Making peace with this parent is the issue for you, because you were the recipient of how he or she was affected. You lived the effects. It is not necessary to debate their existence; it is only important to understand them as they have affected your relationship with this parent. If the non-alcoholic parent remains in denial, it is not your responsibility to overcome it in order to change the non-alcoholic's perception.

One way to avoid the denial trap is to be specific about which feelings, behaviors, or relationship issues you need to make peace about with your non-alcoholic parent. Make lists similar to the ones mentioned earlier in this chapter. Do not be surprised if you have totally different issues with the non-alcoholic parent. Also, do not be surprised with how many you may have. It may seem that you have all of the issues. It is not uncommon for the adult child to feel that the non-alcoholic parent is exempt from the need to make peace. Just because you need to make peace with this parent does not mean that the parent did not do a good job, nor does it mean that you have a bad relationship with this parent. It does indicate that your growth will include all people and issues that are a part of you. Making peace with all parts of you includes making peace with all parts of your family.

Unavailable Parents

Although making peace with your inner parents is the major part of making peace with your parents, some adult children will want to improve relationships with the actual parents. Adult children who have access to the parents can attempt this. Others cannot.

Adult children in this situation will not be able to make peace with the actual parent. As painful as this may be, the adult child still can make peace with the inner parent. The adult child in this situation will need to make peace with the memories associated with the unavailable parent. It is important not to spend energy needed for growth on self-criticism or regret that you should have said something when you had the chance. If you cannot change that now, what can you do? You can express your feelings to yourself, share them with others, share them with a remaining parent or relative that you do have contact with, and set your mind and memories to rest.

Sometimes it will help to write down your feelings about your unavailable parent. Although you do not have contact with the parent, write a letter to them stating all of the things that you would have said if you had had the chance. Putting your feelings on paper can help you to clarify some of them. Some adult children will find this a difficult task to do. Others may write the letter and then discard it. Some adult children may find comfort in sharing their letter with someone close to them or someone who was close to the parent. In this way the adult child knows that at least one other person knows what they would have said to the parent.

Finally, issues with unavailable parents may be accompanied with other concerns besides the alcoholism. The adult child will need to address these as well. These can include abandonment, an early death, divorce or other separation issues.

The Recovering Parent

Adult children of alcoholics who have a recovering parent still can be in need of making peace with this parent. Recovery increases the possibility of improving parent-child relationships, but it does not guarantee it. Many of the issues common to all alcoholic parents will remain inside the adult child, and these issues will require inner healing. Recovering parents can make the present much better, but past issues can linger. Parental recovery can help the adult child with these past issues if both the parent and the adult child are willing to communicate.

Normally, communication with the alcoholic parent is a major problem for adult children. With recovering alcoholic parents, however, it may be the adult child who does not want to talk about the alcoholism or related incidents. Many recovering alcoholics have expressed concern that they would like to improve the relationship with their adult children. They realize that they had a negative impact on their children and would like to work on these issues. When they attempt to converse with their adult children, however, the adult children may say, "No, I wasn't bothered" or "It's OK now" and not want to discuss alcoholism. When this happens, the alcoholic parent is now in the same position the adult children were in when the alcoholic was drinking. It may be the adult child who is now denying any effects.

Adult children of recovering parents must have realistic expectations about recovery. That the alcoholic is recovering does not mean that automatically you are recovering. Just as you cannot recover for an alcoholic parent, the alcoholic cannot recover for you.

Many of the issues for adult children developed over a period of years and will require time and energy to overcome in recovery. To expect expedient recovery for both the alcoholic parent and the adult child on all issues is unrealistic.

Another consideration with recovering parents is not to avoid making peace with your inner parent. There can be a tendency for this to happen. Even though the actual parent is recovering and the adult child begins to work with this parent, inner parent issues will still remain.

Again, make peace with your inner parent. Do not attempt to make peace with the actual parent over current issues and expect that past inner issues will be eliminated. The adult child with a recovering parent has the potential to make peace with both the inner and actual parent, but not all recovering parents and their adult children will be able to do this. Make peace with your inner parent.

Finally, do not put all of your eggs in one basket. Do not become swept up in the recovering parent because you are so pleased with him or her. What about the other parent? Are you continuing to ignore this parent and your issues with them? You could find yourself getting closer to the recovering alcoholic parent and farther away from the non-alcoholic parent. If this occurs, you will find that although you thought you were making peace with your parents, you have not. Make peace with both of your parents to achieve a singular goal, that of making peace with your inner parents.

Forgiveness

How well you can make peace with your parents will depend upon your ability to forgive. Many of your issues and feelings will not be resolved in face-to-face communication with your parents. Forgiveness comes from within. Forgiveness is the key to achieving inner peace. Without it, resentment, anger and guilt can remain. If you truly forgive someone, you no longer resent their behavior. You no longer are angry.

In the following vignette, Paul, a son of an alcoholic father shares his feelings about his experiences and his efforts to forgive.

PAUL'S STORY

I did not become aware of my father's alcohol addiction until I was 26 years old. Throughout my childhood and adolescence,

*all that I knew was that my father was an angry and abusive
man. He seemed to be yelling most of the time. I never knew
how long he would be civil until something clicked inside of
him and he became mean again.*

*As the years went by, his behavior had its effect on me. I
became very passive and turned my anger on myself. It became
difficult for me to trust others or myself. I lost touch with my
feelings. People often wondered why I was so quiet all of the
time. I found it difficult to share what was going on inside of me
because I really didn't believe that it would matter to anybody.*

*By the time I graduated from high school it had reached the
point where I would no longer laugh out loud. Instead, my body
would shake with laughter when something was funny, but no
sound would come out of me.*

*I became very self-conscious about my body. I wanted to
learn how to dance, but I felt so awkward whenever I tried. A
voice from inside kept reminding me that I was sure to fail. I
eventually learned how to dance with a partner, but I still find
it too painful to dance alone. This lack of confidence, which was
brought on by continual criticism, eventually took its toll in my
academic studies. I never came anywhere near my potential.*

*When I was 26 years old, I was finally able to pinpoint my
father's problem. My brother-in-law took me to a couple of AA
meetings and helped me to identify my father's alcohol
addiction. My father has yet to get help for himself, but that has
not held me back in my own recovery.*

*I think that the most important part of my healing process
was learning about forgiveness from the heart. By the time I
reached 28 years of age, I had become quite miserable. All of
the anger towards my father, which I had stored up over the
years, was getting the best of me. In desperation, I agreed to
counsel with an older priest who was himself a recovering
alcoholic. This man showed me the way out of darkness. For
that help, I will be eternally grateful to him.*

*In his wisdom, he knew how much damage I was doing to
myself by nurturing my own resentment. He taught me about
the healing power of forgiveness from the heart. Resentment
does nothing but keep alive the pain in our hearts. Forgiveness
is the letting go of our resentment, so that the pain can die away.
The critical factor is that it does take some time to become
emotionally ready to forgive.*

First, we need to decide to forgive. Then, we need to sincerely want it to happen. In doing this, a steady diet of prayer for it to happen can yield some dramatic results.

In the seven years which have now passed, I have learned an invaluable lesson. Forgiving my father opened my eyes to enable me to see that good had come out of my experience of being a child of an alcoholic parent. Adversity in life will either bring out the best or the worst in us. The decision is ours to make, either consciously or subconsciously. A great number of personal qualities which have made me a better human being and priest are a direct result of my experience in an alcoholic family. They have made me as the saying states a "wounded-healer."

Father Paul
Pittsburgh, PA

Forgiveness may be your best indicator of growth and your best asset for future growth. How well you have forgiven can tell you how much you have let go.

Each adult child must establish his or her own formula to achieve forgiveness. Included might be letting go of a resentment over a particular behavior, feeling abandoned, blaming your parents, wanting things to be different, feeling deprived compared to other children, not having an ideal family or feeling that your parents are responsible for your problems today. It is doubtful that someone will come and take these feelings and issues away. You will need to find a process that will allow you to let go. You do not have to resolve them all. Accept that you cannot change every feeling, and learn to accept the ones you cannot change. You can learn to forgive even if others in your family cannot. There is no law that prohibits self-growth, only human barriers.

Making Peace with Your Siblings

Are all of the adult children in your family children of alcoholics? You may think so, but they may not. If you had to work through your denial, implications and feelings about being an adult child, so do they. You may not all arrive at the same conclusion or agreement about the parental drinking and its effects on you. Making peace with your siblings does not mean that your siblings must agree with you. You have your perception and they have theirs.

Adult children will need to make peace with their own experiences. Often the adult child will feel that the siblings not only must make peace as well, but also that all of the siblings must be in agreement and be mutually supportive. Waiting for this to occur will delay your recovery. It is not necessary for your siblings to validate your perceptions prior to your starting recovery. It would be nice to have this support, but it is highly unlikely. With or without your siblings you can recover.

Making peace with your siblings will depend upon many factors. How well you get along with each other is one of these. Many adult children can remember the silent support that existed among the children. In large families not all of the siblings may have been close, but you may have been close to a particular brother or sister who helped you. On the other hand, some research indicates that siblings in alcoholic families are more distant and argue more than siblings in non-alcoholic families (Wilson, 1978). This be may caused by several factors.

The stress in the family can create stress in the children. Marital discord could have forced the children to take sides with the parents, and thus divide the siblings. Making peace with your siblings can therefore depend upon the type of relationship between you, differences in perceptions, degree of denial, willingness to communicate and their desire to make peace for themselves.

Do not allow any of these issues to deter you from making peace with them. Do not get involved in a debate about whether or not the parent actually was alcoholic. To you the parent was, or you would not consider yourself to be an adult child. Remember, too, that your willingness to recover can be a threat to them, but your recovery is not a betrayal of your relationship. Remember, however, when you say something about your parent, you are also talking about their parent, too. The one thing that siblings share is the parent, but they do not share the same perceptions.

Another precaution is not to allow yourself to be put into a position by your siblings to do an intervention on your parents or the alcoholic. Since you are the one who is recovering from exposure to alcoholism, your siblings may look to you to lead the way for all of them. They may try to make you feel that it is your responsibility to intervene with the parents, especially since you "now know so much about alcoholism". If they are so interested in parental recovery, enlist their aid. Do not allow your recovery to be used against you or to manipulate you.

Making inner peace with your siblings requires you to make peace with the common history that you share. Make peace with all of your sibling behaviors, not merely those that are alcohol related. Be at peace with all of the times that you have shared. Remember that those who know you most may be the most likely to resist your change.

Recovery may require you to take on a new role, one that is unfamiliar to your siblings. Be sure that you have made peace with your inner siblings before you take your new role to your siblings by birth. They may well resist, and you must be prepared in order to avoid emotional relapse.

If you and your siblings do not agree on the alcoholism of the parent, preserve your relationship nonetheless. There are other things that you can share besides parental alcoholism. It may have dominated your childhood relationships, but it need not dominate your adult ones. Accept them for who they are. Accept your own changes, and do not try to change them. Establish your inner peace about your siblings. If you and your siblings are not able to get closer on the parental alcoholism issue, settle for a peaceful co-existence and try getting closer on other issues.

Making Peace with Your Spouse

This part of making peace with your family is concerned with your family of procreation, rather than the family into which you were born. A major determinant of how your own family is affected, however, will be how much of the negative influences of your past you have carried knowingly and unknowingly into your new family. Ironically, many adult children will be determined that their family will be different, only to find themselves repeating many of the behaviors that they witnessed between their parents or that they endured as a child. Obviously, as a child you were not a spouse, but you witnessed spouse behavior between your parents. Thus your ideas come from the role model of marriage that you observed.

How and under what conditions being an adult child may affect your spouse relationship will vary. Some of the common concerns will focus on the ability to be close to someone, on your expectations about being a spouse, on carrying unfinished business into your marriage or on substance-abuse problems by you or your spouse.

Certainly your ability to be close will be a major factor in your spouse relationship; it also will be a major factor in making peace with your spouse. Making peace with your spouse may be necessary if you have carried unfinished business into your marriage.

Unfinished business with others cannot be resolved by taking it out on your spouse. Your spouse is the one who is there, however, and often becomes the verbal recipient of statements that should be made to someone else. Additionally, a problem might arise because the adult child feels that the spouse should understand him or her better.

One of the most common problems in all spouse relationships is the inability to communicate. Adult children of alcoholics who internalize the family norms of "don't talk, don't trust or don't feel" identified by Claudia Black (1982) may be especially vulnerable to this problem. Expecting to have a healthy relationship with your spouse or wanting your spouse to understand you better when you display the above behaviors is unrealistic. Neither should you expect your spouse to accept you as you are if you are an unhealthy adult child. Would you want to live with you? Do not use your adult child status as an excuse not to grow in your relationship.

Holding onto negative patterns will develop negative patterns in your current relationship. On the other hand there may be adult children who feel that they married for the wrong reasons. Either way, the adult child may feel that he or she needs to make peace with his or her spouse.

If you are having relationship problems with your spouse, assess your level of recovery as an adult child first. Your level of recovery may be related to your degree of relationship problems.

Rather than engage in premature closure of your relationship as your only alternative, try dealing with your adult children issues first. In this manner you will have a clearer understanding of which issues are relationship issues and which ones may be more related to unresolved adult children issues. Trying to clear up relationship issues prior to making peace with your adult children status will impede and undermine your relationship efforts. It makes more sense to work on one before the other, particularly if one might be related to the other. As part of your recovery do not be hesitant to seek help in areas other than adult childrens' concerns. If you are having spouse relationship problems, try marital counseling. If you want to improve your communication abilities, seek intervention for this skill. Healthy relationships require energy invested in a variety of areas, sometimes simultaneously.

Finally, do not expect your spouse to deliver you from your unhappy past. This is not your spouse's responsibility. You may feel that your spouse relationship and marriage was exactly what you needed to make your life complete, to provide you with the happiness that you did not have, but do not expect your spouse to be all things to you. Not only is this too much to ask of anyone, but also it is an unrealistic expectation. On the other hand, if you are an adult child who is always helping others, do not try to deliver your spouse from his or her past. Do not allow your habits to impede your abilities or desire to have a healthy relationship; it is a noble goal.

Making Peace with Your Children

Will you parent your children the way you were parented? Why would an adult child need to make peace with his or her children? There are several factors that having children will raise for adult children. One of the most obvious of these is that raising children often will put you into contact with your own childhood. Your children will engage in some of the same behaviors you did. Their behaviors can remind you of your childhood. Your parenting skills can remind you of your parents. Your children will require nurturing and understanding that you may not have received and will challenge your ability to learn these behaviors.

Rearing children is stressful for all adults, but it may be particularly stressful for those adult children who do not handle stress well. Because of their unusual childhoods many adult children may be unaware of normal human development in children and thus find normal behavior to be stressful.

Studies indicate, for example, that an adult child has higher expectations of compliant behavior in children than do adults of non-alcoholic parents. The adult child's understanding of children may come from his or her childhood, even though the adult child realizes that the childhood was not healthy. Many adult children were extremely compliant and mature as children, and they expect their own children to be the same. They watch their children engaging in normal behavior, and think "I would not have dared to do that". The criterion for what is normal, however, is their own childhood. Are adult children saying that they want their children to behave as they did, even though they admit that they were raised under less than ideal conditions?

Making peace with your children can mean many things to the adult child. It means making peace with your own childhood because your children will remind you of it. It means allowing your children to be normal and not to repeat your childhood. It means not being jealous that your children have it better than you did. It means not resenting your children because they do not understand your childhood or your adult child status. To your children, you are a parent first and an adult child second. You need to be a healthy parent for them, which being a healthy adult child will help you to accomplish.

Other issues that may arise with your children can be over your parents, who are their grandparents. What kinds of messages will you convey to them about their grandparents? Another issue may develop if your children choose to drink alcohol. Will you ask them to promise never to drink? Will you caution them or offer guidance about alcoholism, or will you convey to them a feeling that substance use or abuse is not a subject that they can talk about with you?

Whatever issues having children will raise for you, remember that this is their childhood, not yours. Be at peace with their childhood. Do not expect your children to meet your needs disproportionately. Many adult children feel that they parented their parents. Do not ask your children to do this for you. Healthy families require healthy fulfillment of roles, so be a healthy parent and allow your children to develop into healthy children.

Making peace with your family occurs internally and externally. It involves making peace with the family you were born into and the family that you may start. Making peace with your family can be an extension of making peace with yourself. It must be an adjunct to your own growth, however, not a substitute. If you are able to make peace with your family, you have taken a giant step towards letting go in order to grow.

For many adult children, making peace with their family will allow them to achieve an emotionally neutral position from which genuine growth can begin. It will allow the adult child to go forward without constantly needing to look back. Making peace with reality, with yourself and your family will prepare you for the kind of growth that will truly improve your life.

The core of this growth will become not only the peace that you have made by learning to let go, but also your ability to achieve positive emotional intimacy in order to grow.

6

Beyond Letting Go: Achieving Positive Emotional Intimacy

Letting go of the past and of the many emotionally associated issues will allow the adult child to free energy that now can be used to develop new skills. For many adult children the most important part of themselves they would like to develop is the ability to achieve positive emotional intimacy with others.

The adult child who has worked through all of the types and phases of making peace is ready to improve life, but not all adult children will try. Some adult children will be able to let go of the past but go no further. Others will not be able to let go and will retain many of their original feelings and childhood experiences. Still others will eagerly embrace the opportunity to become the type of person they have always wanted to be. The core of their growth will be dependent upon their ability to achieve positive emotional intimacy in their lives.

It is commonly thought that many adult children of alcoholics have difficulty achieving intimacy. What is more intimate than living with an alcoholic? You know the alcoholic and the effects on family members exceptionally well, but this type of intimacy is negative. Negative emotional intimacy develops from exceptionally close contact with people who affect one in a detrimental fashion. It requires the recipient to endure and often to rationalize the inappropriate emotional consequences. It leads to impairing the development of positive emotional intimacy. Negative emotional intimacy can be the unintended consequence that affects adults who were reared in alcoholic homes. Not only are these adults negatively affected by the parental alcoholism, but also their perceptions of intimacy are distorted. For example, the adult child may believe it more appropriate to share his or her feelings with strangers or casual friends than to share them in an intimate relationship. The adult child enters marriage with the idea that you do not share information and feelings with your spouse, only outside of the marriage, that one should not share intimacy within the family. Often this form of intimacy dominates adult children.

The intimacy that is difficult for adult children of alcoholics to achieve is positive emotional intimacy. This type of intimacy is shared and results in positive outcomes. It allows for the growth and development of the adult child and improves the quality of life.

However, negative emotional intimacy is used to control others. Positive emotional intimacy involves growing with others such as your spouse, children, parents, friends, relatives or the person whom you are dating. Emotional intimacy is not limited to lovers. It is part of every relationship that involves loving and being loved.

Achieving positive emotional intimacy requires changing awareness into actions. A significant portion of the journey of recovery is consumed in self-discovery. This allows for a better understanding by the adult child. Once the levels of awareness have been raised, however, growth must be active if it is to continue. The adult child will need to begin to practice and live the desired changes. Not all adult children will need the same transition. Some will already be more emotionally content in their adult lives than others. For those who have been emotionally isolated, allowing themselves to achieve positive emotional intimacy will be a major undertaking. Old habits will be hard to abandon. For the isolated adult child, closeness was associated with pain and vulnerability. It will be difficult to accept that it can be associated with growth.

The difficulty of achieving positive emotional intimacy will be dependent upon two factors: the degree of current emotional satisfaction; how strongly the barriers to achieving emotional intimacy are maintained.

Table 6.1

Level of Emotional Satisfaction Found Among Adult Children of Alcoholics and Adult Children of Non-Alcoholic Parents

Level of Satisfaction	Non-ACoA (n=488)	ACoA (n=502)
Above average	48.4%	35.5%
Average	37.7	42.4
Below Average	13.9	22.1
	100.0%	100.0%

At this stage of your life, how emotionally satisfied are you? Adult children who are emotionally satisfied have a foundation upon which to grow that may not be available to those less satisfied. In Table 6.1 adult children of alcoholics are compared to adult children of non-alcoholic parents for their levels of emotional satisfaction (see Table 6.1).

Table 6.1 indicates that adults of non-alcoholic parents have higher levels of emotional satisfaction than adult children of alcoholics. However, more than one third of adult children of alcoholics indicated that they were more than emotionally satisfied with their lives. This finding supports the often repeated assumptions in this book that all adult children are not the same, that they are not all affected the same, that not all adult children feel the same degree of negative feelings, and that not all adult children will need to recover to the same extent.

On the other hand, Table 6.1 indicates that the majority of adult children of alcoholics do not fall into the above average levels of emotional satisfaction. Therefore, many adult children of alcoholics may want to improve the quality of their levels of emotional satisfaction.

If you want to achieve positive emotional intimacy but you cannot, what keeps you from accomplishing your goals? You may possess barriers which have kept you locked into patterns that impede the development of healthy intimate relationships. You may or may not be aware of these barriers. Although all adults may have some difficulty with intimate relationships, adult children of alcoholics can possess characteristics that will make them exceptionally susceptible to these problems.

These characteristics include low self-esteem, problems over control, inability to trust others, triangulation, compassion, fatigue, maintaining an emotional diet, the inability to receive and macro-responsibility. The adult child who wants to develop positive emotional intimacy will need to overcome these barriers. He or she will need to make a transition from remaining behind these barriers which prohibit growth to developing positive interaction characteristics that will improve relationships. The following is a discussion of each of these barriers and the transition that is needed.

Low Self-Esteem
Can Become High Self-Esteem

Adult children may be susceptible to low self-esteem problems for several reasons.

1. Their interests in the family may have been subjugated to a low level because of the dominating effect of alcoholism.
2. They may have been falsely accused of creating the family dysfunction.
3. They may have felt highly stigmatized by the alcoholism and thus not as good as others.
4. Their environment did not foster the development of healthy role models and thus they may not have experienced close relationships.

Whatever the causes, many adult children are left with low self-esteem. This may or may not be easily noticeable to others. Many adult children are extremely competent in several areas which mask their insecurities in relationships, but these competencies, no matter how significant, cannot help them to create positive emotional intimacy. Learning to be close and allowing others to get close requires internal growth, not external accomplishments.

Establishing positive intimacy begins with yourself. If you do not like and love yourself, why should anyone else? It is difficult to get close to other people when you do not like what you are offering. Adult children who have a low opinion of themselves will need to raise their levels of self-esteem to establish healthy relationships. This process includes an internal evaluation of your qualities and assets. It also can include placing yourself in a position where you can succeed, getting reinforced for your successes and thus raise your self-esteem. Let's face it, positive accomplishments will help you, too, in addition to your internal growth.

If you have made peace with reality and with yourself, your self-esteem already should be growing. These two steps in recovery will help to eliminate many unwanted behaviors. Understanding that you have capabilities and qualities to offer others will facilitate raising your opinion of yourself. Do not treat yourself like a second-class citizen, nor allow others to do so. Self-esteem means to respect yourself. Seek out healthy people with whom to establish healthy relationships.

Inability to Trust Can Be Changed to the Ability to Trust

Healthy relationships are built on mutual trust. Many adult children of alcoholics only trust themselves. Trusting others is extremely difficult for adults who learned that autonomy was necessary for survival. Adult children of alcoholics can and do trust, but they may not trust when it comes to relationships or intimacy. What undermines all of our relationships, whether between friends, lovers, parents, children or client-counselor, is the degree of trust in that relationship. The type of trust that is so critical concerns the amount of information that is shared.

For example, if I trust you with information about myself, I am trusting that at a later time in our relationship you will not use that information against me. Keeping information about yourself from others is a norm for many adult children. Thus, learning to trust is not only a new behavior, it also requires breaking well established habits for many adult children.

To trust, you need someone who is trustworthy. Adult children will need to use discretion about whom they trust. Do not take an all-or-nothing approach when trusting others. That is, you tell them absolutely everything or nothing at all. Learn to trust yourself with your feelings first. Begin to share your feelings with others by degree. Trust in relationships is established, it is not a given. Establishing trust is an interactive process. Adult children who cannot trust others will never fully interact with others who are trustworthy.

Do not rob yourself of healthy relationships because of your inability to trust yourself and others. Growth is a process of learning new behaviors. Trust yourself that you can learn.

From Triangulation
to Direct Communication

Triangulation is the process of never dealing directly with an issue or another person. For example, an adult child who needs to confront another person or an issue does so by indirect means only. Rather than communicating directly, the adult child finds an external focal point through which to channel all communication. If the adult child needs to relate to another person, he or she uses an external excuse in order to avoid direct communication.

This behavior may be familiar to many adult children because in childhood they may have been the external focal point for the relationship between their parents. Thus, the communication pattern was learned by the adult child who was a participant in the parents' communication triangle.

Triangulation is a barrier to achieving positive emotional intimacy because true feelings are never expressed directly. The adult child who suffers from triangulation must learn new communication skills. These skills will allow the adult child to handle relationship issues directly, which will improve the quality of the relationships and reduce the amount of "hidden" messages that are contained in triangulated interaction patterns.

A characteristic of triangulation is finding excuses which serve the purpose of avoiding situations or needed communications. When problems arise between an adult child and another person, the adult child can choose to express feelings directly or choose to pretend that something or someone prohibits dealing with the problem.

An example of this might be that an adult child and a significant other need to communicate about a particular problem. The adult child knows this but states that "The weekend is coming and I don't want to upset the other person." Other common triangulation statements are "We tried that before and it didn't work, so why try it again"? or "I know that we should deal with this, but it isn't the right time."

Triangulation means putting your feelings second to some external focal point. The adult child must realize that positive emotional intimacy cannot be achieved indirectly. It requires open and direct communication, so do not put unnecessary emotional barriers in your way.

Triangulation is a form of denial. It denies you the opportunity to grow at the expense of maintaining negative interaction patterns.

From Over-control to the Proper Amount of Control

It has been stated that many adult children have problems with control. Although taking control of situations in childhood may have been necessary for adult children of alcoholics, demanding too much control may become a liability in adult relationships. What is it, however, that some adult children want to control? Problems of over-control can create three types of barriers to achieving intimacy.

One type of control problem can be found in adult children who feel a need to control situations. They constantly feel they need to be in charge or to be the center of all activities. Although this behavior may have its origins in childhood, from having to take charge of chaotic alcoholic situations, it will become problematic not only for the adult child, but also for those around the adult child.

Two problems are likely to arise. One, the adult child may initially welcome or feel the need to be in charge. However, this same adult child later may resent having to do everything. The second problem is the development of expectations by others that the adult child must be in control at the expense of the contributions of others.

Adult children with situational control problems will need to learn to let others contribute, that they do not have to do everything themselves, and that others' contributions can be just as beneficial as theirs. Finally, adult children will need to learn to become comfortable in situations where they are not in charge or where they are the center of attention. Learning to listen to others and allowing yourself to become part of a group, rather than controlling the group will facilitate your growth.

A second type of control problem exists for those adult children who need to control relationships. They feel that if they control a relationship, it is a comfortable relationship, but is it a healthy one? Often the need to control a relationship by the adult child is seen as a way to minimize relationship problems, unexpected behaviors and to create guarantees that the person will accept any and all of your behaviors.

Many adult children are very good in "parenting roles" and often carry these into their adult relationships. When this happens, they knowingly or unknowingly treat the other person as if it was a parent-child relationship. They may be a very loving "parent", but that is appropriate only in parenting relationships. The adult child does not need to relinquish all control in a relationship, however: he or she can keep 50% as opposed to 75%. Healthy relationships require risk, energy and commitment, rather than one person controlling all of the behaviors and emotions for two persons. The adult child who expects another person to accept the controlling behavior is asking for the other person to become co-dependent. A controlled relationship is a co-dependent relationship.

The third type of control problem is found in the emotions of the adult child. That is, the adult child wants to maintain control over emotions by never losing control or allowing himself or herself to become too emotional. Again, this may be a normal response from childhood, where getting emotionally expressive may have been met with pain, but in adulthood it will prohibit the adult child from experiencing all that relationships have to give. You may consider your self-control behavior as an asset, but others in a relationship will feel that you never open up, that you are difficult to understand or that they cannot get close to you emotionally.

If you want to be loved, it helps to be loving. Suppressing your emotions will suppress your growth. How can you feel joy, happiness, love, grief, or passion if you cannot feel? Do not control your emotions too much, because your emotions are the foundation for your feelings. Without this foundation you may find yourself thinking, "Why can't I feel like other people?" or "I wish I could communicate in my relationship the way they do." Too much control over your emotions results in too little feeling in your relationships.

Releasing controlling behaviors requires risk, energy and time. You will need to become aware of your controlling behavior, find alternative ways to interact when they occur, and accept the contributions of others to your life. It is not easy to give up over-control, but maintaining it means that you give up improving your relationships.

Macro-responsibility Can Become Reasonable Responsibility

Do you often feel responsible for things that are beyond your control? Do you feel guilty unnecessarily? You may have feelings of "macro-responsibility".

This can develop in two forms. One is when you allow yourself to get into positions of too much responsibility in too many areas, thus you over-extend yourself and have too little energy for yourself or your relationships. The other form occurs when you allow yourself to assume responsibility for situations over which you have no control. This can be either a self-imposed sense of responsibility or a sense you allow others to impose on you, such as allowing others to make you feel guilty for their predicaments. This puts you in a position that you feel that you must expend your energy to solve everyone else's problems. After all, if you accept the responsibility, you feel that you must find the solution.

Both of these forms of macro-responsibility are barriers to achieving positive emotional intimacy. They will keep you away from intimacy and reduce your available energy for contributing to your own healthy needs. One of the ways to overcome macro-responsibility is to set and to accept limitations.

The adult child must learn to say "no" to some of the requests from others. This is not easy for adult children who feel that they must please everyone or that if they say no, they will no longer be accepted. Knowing your limitations is a part of growth.

You learn that you cannot do everything and that, more importantly, it is not your responsibility.

It reminds me of sitting in front of the TV as a child and listening to Smokey-the-Bear inform me that "only you can prevent forest fires". What a responsibility to lay on a child! I sat in the backyard for an entire summer watering the trees. How relieved I was to find out in school that "you" was also plural.

Accepting your limitations also can mean accepting help from others. It allows you to share with others and allows for them to share with you. It is the basis for healthy relationships. Often adult children with overly-developed senses of responsibility will feel that it is their obligation to make relationships work. Therefore, they take on too much emotional responsibility in a relationship and often allow themselves to be used. In the end they blame themselves for not doing more if the relationship fails. This kind of behavior will not produce healthy relationships, whether between friends, lovers, spouses or parents and their children.

The adult child owes a healthy sense of responsibility to himself or herself. Positive emotional intimacy can be achieved through balance, not through over-extending yourself. The adult child will need to learn that limitations not only are acceptable but a normal part of healthy relationships. Contrary to your belief, you cannot be all things to all people. You can be, however, the best at those things that you can do and you can allow yourself to accept the best in others.

Compassion Fatigue Can Be Changed to Feeling Again

Compassion fatigue occurs as a result of being emotionally drained. Many adult children have given so much or have endured so much emotionally as children that they find it difficult as an adult to care about their feelings or about others. Often they confide that they pretend to feel what others do, but actually they feel nothing. They feel nothing now because they felt too much previously.

Another form of compassion fatigue is wanting to feel but not knowing how. The adult child wants to feel, but experiences low levels of energy because so much energy was previously drained.

Suffering from compassion fatigue will inhibit the development of positive emotional intimacy. The adult child is simply too handicapped emotionally to allow for the true expression of feelings. Thus many of them go through the emotions of pretending to feel, but at the same time feel empty. This is caused by emotional exhaustion and overload, hence, fatigue.

Those adult children suffering from compassion fatigue will need to disengage from situations that are too emotionally draining. They will need to free up energy that is consumed on negative issues in order to use their energy for positive growth. It will require learning to care about the appropriate issues and allowing yourself to express and receive positive feelings. It is not easy to overcome compassion fatigue, because one of the major characteristics for people who have survived negative experiences is a low level of energy. The adult child will need to produce energy in order to accept his or her feelings. Compassion fatigue will not be overcome at once. Do not try to do so, because you will only create more fatigue in trying, but it can be overcome in small energy increments. Invest your energy in feeling the positive things in your life.

Going Off That Emotional Diet

Engaging in most of the above barriers to achieving positive emotional intimacy will put you on an "emotional diet", that is, you will not allow certain emotions to enter your whole being. You will allow yourself only to feel or express a very limited range of emotions.

For example, our range of emotions could be analogous to a piano keyboard. We are born with an emotional range of 88 keys. Many adult children allow previous experiences to prevent them from playing more than a few emotional keys, thus they try not to get too high or too low. Although this may appear to be a logical way to manage your emotions, it also keeps you from fully experiencing your emotional capabilities.

Also, it can affect your relationships in two ways. The first is that you will not be able to receive many emotions given by others at the level that they are sent. For example, someone sends you his or her 67th key of joy. For years you have responded only to all emotions from a range of keys numbered 30 to 50, however, so you are unable to meet this emotion at the level from which it was sent. The second problem is that you will have a very limited range from which to send emotions.

It will be difficult to maintain a relationship around a healthy person, one who uses all of the keyboard, when you are limited in your responses and messages. An emotional diet is one diet that you do not need to maintain. Unlike other diets, remaining on this one will inhibit your growth and not improve your self-image.

The adult child who is on an emotional diet will find it hard to let go and experience love, warmth, joy and happiness offered by others. He or she often will wonder why others seem to enjoy themselves more or have more meaningful relationships. A full relationship requires a total capability to enjoy it, whether with friends, lovers, your children, your spouse or your parents. The ability to begin a full relationship begins with yourself. You must be able to acknowledge and share all of your feelings. If you limit yourself emotionally by remaining on an emotional diet, you will limit your relationships.

The Inability To Receive Can Become The Ability To Receive

Of all of the barriers to achieving positive emotional intimacy, the inability to receive may be the greatest for adult children of alcoholics. This is because many adult children are excellent "givers" but poor "receivers". Healthy relationships are built on a give-and-take basis.

The adult child who wants to grow is often surprised to find out that he or she does not have the ability to receive from others. When put into a receiving situation, they often are uncomfortable. For example, what do you do when someone pays you a compliment? Do you discount it by saying, "Oh, this old thing, I got it on sale," or do you accept the compliment and say, "Thank you"?

There is a great difference between interdependence and co-dependence. Interdependence is the ability to give and receive and still maintain your own identity. Co-dependence is based on one of the participants giving more than the other, and yet the giver takes on the identity of the receiver.

Developing your ability to receive will develop your ability to grow. One facilitates the other. You will be able to accept the feelings offered by those who love you. You will be able to accept your own feelings and growth. You will become balanced. A healthy person can give 50% in a relationship and receive 50% in a relationship. This means that for adult children of alcoholics who are 75% givers, change is needed. Many adult children are not even aware of their ability to receive. It is a commodity that has not been tested. The adult child may need to back off on giving and learn to grow as a receiver. If you are in a 75% relationship, you are likely to overwhelm the other person.

If the other person is healthy, he or she normally will withdraw when overwhelmed. Unfortunately, what most adult children givers then do is come on stronger and try to fix the relationship by giving still more, thus contributing further to overwhelming the other person.

Transforming the above barriers will facilitate the adult child in achieving positive emotional intimacy. Maintaining these barriers will make it extremely difficult for the adult child to become the type of person he or she would like to become. These barriers are unnecessary burdens from the past that will affect adult relationships. These burdens keep the adult child out of emotional balance. The healthy adult child will need to maintain an emotional balance in his or her life. Growth is a process of the integration of all of our emotions. Maintaining balance by acknowledging and working through all of your emotions is a vital part of this process. Although not all adult children will use the same approaches to achieving balance, the following suggestions may help.

Affirm your positive assets.

Be positive about yourself.

Learn to like yourself.

Trust your feelings; they will not betray you.

Be more direct and open with your feelings and communications with others.

Do not put unneccesary obstacles or excuses in the paths of your relationships.

Practice giving up control and allow others to contribute to situations and relationships.

Do not deny your emotions.

Share responsibility when appropriate.

Accept your physical and emotional limitations.

Learn to say "no".

Replenish your energy by taking time for yourself.

Express positive emotions that usually are controlled.

Be willing to receive positively from others.

Throughout this entire book, the process of growth has been discussed. Whether this growth involves accepting your past, yourself, your parents or relationships, it has always been directed towards improving the quality of your life. As indicated early in the book and again in the research findings, the area in which adult children have indicated the greatest desire for growth has been in their personal relationships.

If the lives of adult children are going to improve, the degree to which they can achieve positive emotional intimacy will be the determining factor. A negative childhood is no longer the issue once you become an adult. The primary concern at that point is whether or not you can achieve a positive adulthood. The liabilities of childhood must not rob you of your adulthood. You have a choice which will allow you to go and grow beyond childhood.

You *can* become a healthy adult, but you do not, nor can you, do this alone. Remember, when you were alone as a child, you could not improve your situation; you could only survive it. Now that you are an adult, it is time to be more than a survivor. It is time to go beyond survival. It is a challenge to your human spirit that tells you that now is the time. Now that you have survived, now that you have endured, now that you no longer need to put yourself second, now it is your time. Now it is your turn.

Do not turn away from it, but rather turn towards it. The fully recovering adult child not only is aware of the past, but also of his or her present status. He or she is aware that recovery is an ongoing process that allows the individual to go beyond the past.

Recovering is not limited to understanding only the past, because there are no limits in recovering. Only you can become the "limiter". Only your own emotional barriers will impede your recovery.

The adult child who can achieve positive emotional intimacy will go beyond letting go. In fact, he or she will go beyond the statment that "I am an adult child and I am becoming . . ."

Being an adult child will no longer be the master status identity. Being a child of an alcoholic will no longer be the most dominant part of the adult. The recovering adult child will be able to put alcoholism in its proper perspective in his or her life. No longer will it control the adult child. The recovering adult child will be in control of his or her life and of all of his or her life experiences.

Letting go will lead to such recovering statements as, "I am content, happy, joyful, forgiving, loving, loved, growing, and I am an adult child of an alcoholic."

Appendix

The National Adult Children of Alcoholics research study was conducted by Robert J. Ackerman, Ph.D., of the Sociology Department at Indiana University of Pennsylvania under the Faculty Research Associate Program. This study was an exploratory descriptive study designed to assess differences in personality characteristics reported in adult children of alcoholics from adult children of non-alcoholic parents. An assessment instrument, based on these differences, will be developed from this study.

Data was gathered by using the survey method of a self-administered questionnaire. Approximately 1,000 adults participated in the study of which half came from alcoholic families. The data was collected from 38 states. Adult children were self-identified and did not come from a clinical population, but from adult children of alcoholics in general. Only 20% of the adult children of alcoholics in this study received any treatment related to being an adult child of an alcoholic.

In addition to studying personality characteristics of adult children this study also focused on race, gender, age, siblings, child abuse and type of alcoholic behaviors as they relate to adult children of alcoholics. Other areas studied included assessments of family stability, major areas of concerns for adult children of alcoholics, degree of impact of alcoholism on adult children and overall levels of emotional statisfaction in adulthood.

Bibliography

Ackerman, Nathan W. *The Psychodynamics of Family Life: Diagnosis and Treatment of Family Relationships.* Basic Books, New York, NY, 1958.

Ackerman, Robert J. "The National Adult Children of Alcoholics Research Study" Indiana University of Pennsylvania, Indiana, PA, 1987.

Ackerman, Robert J. *Same House, Different Homes.* Health Communications, Pompano Beach, FL, 1987.

Ackerman, Robert J. *Growing in the Shadow.* Health Communications, Pompano Beach, FL, 1986.

Ackerman, Robert J. *Children of Alcoholics.* Learning Publications, Holmes Beach, FL, 1983.

Anthony, James. in "Resilient Children" by Maya Pines, *American Educator,* Fall, 1984.

Baldwin, Bruce D. *It's All in Your Head: Lifestyle Management Strategies for Busy People.* Direction Dynamics, Wilmington, NC, 1985.

Black, Claudia. *It Will Never Happen to Me.* M.A.C. Publishing, Denver, CO, 1982.

Bloomfield, Harold and Leonard Felder. *Making Peace with Your Parents.* Ballantine, New York, NY, 1985.

Brenner, Avis. *Helping Children Cope with Stress.* Lexington Books, Lexington, MA, 1984.

Cork, Margaret R. *The Forgotten Child.* Addiction Research Foundation, Ontario, Canada, 1969.

Erikson, E. H. *Childhood and Society.* W. W. Norton, New York, NY, 1963.

Garmezy, N. et al. as reported by Eleanor Hoover in *Human Behavior,* April, 1976.

Gil, Elaine. *Outgrowing the Pain*. Launch Press, San Francisco, CA, 1984.

Goodwin, D. W. "Genetics of Alcoholism", *Alcohol Technical Reports*, 12-13, 7-11, 183-84.

Greenleaf, Jael. Presentation at the Regional Children of Alcoholics Conference, sponsored by the U.S. Journal of Drug and Alcohol Dependence, Los Angeles, CA, November, 1984.

Hindman, M. "Children of Alcoholic Parents". *Alcohol World Health and Research*, NIAAA, Winter, 1975-76.

Hoff, Lee Ann. *People in Crisis*. 2nd ed., Addison-Wesley Publishing, Menlo Park, CA, 1984.

Moos, R. and B. Moos. "Process of Recovery from Alcoholism: Comparing Functioning in Families of Alcoholics and Matched Control Families" *Journal of Studies on Alcohol*, 45(2), 111-118, 1984.

Morehouse, Ellen and Tarpley Richards. "An Examination of Dysfunctional Latency Age Children of Alcoholic Parents and Problems in Intervention". *Journal of Children in Contemporary Society*, 15(1), 1982.

Obuchowska, I. "Emotional Contact with the Mother as a Social Compensatory Factor in Children of Alcoholics". *International Mental Health Research Newsletter*, 16(4), 2:4, 1974.

Perrin, Thomas. *I Am An Adult Child of An Alcoholic*. Thomas W. Perrin, 1984.

Peter, Lawrence and Raymond Hull. *The Peter Principle*. Bantam Books, New York, NY, 1970.

Satir, Virginia. *Conjoint Family Therapy*. Science and Behavior Books, Palo Alto, CA, 1972.

Segal, Eric. *Love Story*. Avon Books, New York, NY, 1977.

Seixas, Judy and Geraldine Youcha. *Children of Alcoholism*. Crown Publishing, New York, NY, 1985.

Strauss, M. et al. *Behind Closed Doors: Violence in the American Family*. Anchor Press, Garden City, NY, 1980.

Volchok, Susan. "Childhood Labels" *Glamour*, July, 1985.

Volicer, B. et al. "Variation in Length of Time to Development of Alcoholism by Family History of Problem Drinking" *Drug and Alcohol Dependence*, 12(1), 69-83, 1983.

Wegscheider, Sharon et al. *Family Illness: Chemical Dependency*. Nurturing Networks, Crystal, MN, 1978.

Werner, E. "Resilient Offspring of Alcoholics: A Longitudinal Study from Birth to Age 18", *Journal of Studies on Alcohol,* 47(1) 34-40, 1986.

Williams, Carol N. "Differences in Child Care Practices Among Families with Alcoholic Fathers, Alcoholic Mothers, and Two Alcoholic Parents". *Dissertation Abstracts International,* 44(01), 299-A, 1983.

Wilsnack, S. and L. Beckman. *Alcohol Problems in Women.* Guilford Press, New York, NY, 1984.

Wilson, C. and J. Orford. "Children of Alcoholics: Report of a Preliminary Study and Comments on the Literature", *Journal of Studies on Alcohol* 39(1): 121-142, 1978.

Woititz, Janet. *Adult Children of Alcoholics.* Health Communications, Pompano Beach, FL, 1983.